"In this beautifully clear book, Mitchell Ch [ ] biblical witness, showing that the resurrecti [ ] entire narrative. Chase demonstrates that the [ ] confined to the New Testament but is clearly [ ] well. Our hope is for life after death—bodily, resurrected life—and we are reminded in this timely book that this hope is ours in Jesus Christ."

Thomas R. Schreiner, James Buchanan Harrison Professor of New Testament Interpretation, The Southern Baptist Theological Seminary

"In one of the best contributions to the Short Studies in Biblical Theology series to date, Mitchell Chase clearly and succinctly presents what is at the heart of hope set before us in the gospel—unending, embodied, glorious resurrection life on a renewed earth—which is so much more than the hope of going to heaven when we die, anticipating a disembodied existence somewhere away from this earth. Significantly, this book shows how New Testament teaching about bodily resurrection is rooted in Old Testament stories and prophecies, helping readers to connect the dots from Genesis to Revelation."

Nancy Guthrie, Bible teacher; author, *Even Better than Eden*

"'The topic of resurrection hope is dear to my heart,' says Mitchell Chase. And so too for me. As I live out my brief life here on earth, as I grapple with sin and temptation, as I endure pain and sickness, as I say farewell to so many I've loved and lost, the hope that sustains me—the only hope, really—is the death of death and the promise of resurrection. This wonderful book shows how the entirety of Scripture teaches that those who are in Christ can have every confidence that they will rise to everlasting life and everlasting joy in his presence. That makes this a book of encouragement, a book of blessing, and a book of hope."

Tim Challies, author, *Seasons of Sorrow: The Pain of Loss and the Comfort of God*

Resurrection Hope and the Death of Death

Short Studies in Biblical Theology

Edited by Dane C. Ortlund and Miles V. Van Pelt

The City of God and the Goal of Creation, T. Desmond Alexander (2018)

Covenant and God's Purpose for the World, Thomas R. Schreiner (2017)

Divine Blessing and the Fullness of Life in the Presence of God, William R. Osborne (2020)

From Chaos to Cosmos: Creation to New Creation, Sidney Greidanus (2018)

The Kingdom of God and the Glory of the Cross, Patrick Schreiner (2018)

The Lord's Supper as the Sign and Meal of the New Covenant, Guy Prentiss Waters (2019)

Marriage and the Mystery of the Gospel, Ray Ortlund (2016)

The New Creation and the Storyline of Scripture, Frank Thielman (2021)

Redemptive Reversals and the Ironic Overturning of Human Wisdom, G. K. Beale (2019)

Resurrection Hope and the Death of Death, Mitchell L. Chase (2022)

The Royal Priesthood and the Glory of God, David S. Schrock (2022)

The Sabbath as Rest and Hope for the People of God, Guy Prentiss Waters (2022)

The Serpent and the Serpent Slayer, Andrew David Naselli (2020)

The Son of God and the New Creation, Graeme Goldsworthy (2015)

Work and Our Labor in the Lord, James M. Hamilton Jr. (2017)

Resurrection Hope and the Death of Death

Mitchell L. Chase

:: CROSSWAY®

WHEATON, ILLINOIS

Cover design and illustration: Jordan Singer

First printing 2022

Printed in the United States of America

All emphases in Scripture quotations have been added by the author.

Trade paperback ISBN: 978-1-4335-8040-6
ePub ISBN: 978-1-4335-8043-7
PDF ISBN: 978-1-4335-8041-3
Mobipocket ISBN: 978-1-4335-8042-0

Library of Congress Cataloging-in-Publication Data

Names: Chase, Mitchell L., 1983– author.
Title: Resurrection hope and the death of death / Mitchell L. Chase.
Description: Wheaton, Illinois : Crossway, 2022. | Series: Short studies in biblical theology | Includes bibliographical references and index.
Identifiers: LCCN 2021046463 (print) | LCCN 2021046464 (ebook) | ISBN 9781433580406 (trade paperback) | ISBN 9781433580413 (pdf) | ISBN 9781433580420 (mobipocket) | ISBN 9781433580437 (epub)
Subjects: LCSH: Resurrection—Biblical teaching. | Death—Biblical teaching. | Hope—Biblical teaching. | Bible—Criticism, interpretation, etc.
Classification: LCC BS680.R37 C43 2022 (print) | LCC BS680.R37 (ebook) | DDC 232/.5—dc23
LC record available at https://lccn.loc.gov/2021046463
LC ebook record available at https://lccn.loc.gov/2021046464

Crossway is a publishing ministry of Good News Publishers.

BP		31	30	29	28	27	26	25	24	23	22
15	14	13	12	11	10	9	8	7	6	5	4	3	2	1

For Andrew Peterson,
whose music and books portray
the beauty and power of resurrection hope

Contents

Series Preface

Most of us tend to approach the Bible early on in our Christian lives as a vast, cavernous, and largely impenetrable book. We read the text piecemeal, finding golden nuggets of inspiration here and there, but remain unable to plug any given text meaningfully into the overarching storyline. Yet one of the great advances in evangelical biblical scholarship over the past few generations has been the recovery of biblical theology—that is, a renewed appreciation for the Bible as a theologically unified, historically rooted, progressively unfolding, and ultimately Christ-centered narrative of God's covenantal work in our world to redeem sinful humanity.

This renaissance of biblical theology is a blessing, yet little of it has been made available to the general Christian population. The purpose of Short Studies in Biblical Theology is to connect the resurgence of biblical theology at the academic level with everyday believers. Each volume is written by a capable scholar or churchman who is consciously writing in a way that requires no prerequisite theological training of the reader. Instead, any thoughtful Christian disciple can track with and benefit from these books.

Each volume in this series takes a whole-Bible theme and traces it through Scripture. In this way readers not only learn about a given theme but also are given a model for how to read the Bible as a coherent whole.

We have launched this series because we love the Bible, we love the church, and we long for the renewal of biblical theology in the academy to enliven the hearts and minds of Christ's disciples all around the world. As editors, we have found few discoveries more thrilling in life than that of seeing the whole Bible as a unified story of God's gracious acts of redemption, and indeed of seeing the whole Bible as ultimately about Jesus, as he himself testified (Luke 24:27; John 5:39).

The ultimate goal of Short Studies in Biblical Theology is to magnify the Savior and to build up his church—magnifying the Savior through showing how the whole Bible points to him and his gracious rescue of helpless sinners; and building up the church by strengthening believers in their grasp of these life-giving truths.

Dane C. Ortlund and Miles V. Van Pelt

Preface

The purpose of this book is to stir your hope for the life you were made for in Christ. Outwardly we are wasting away (2 Cor. 4:16), but that is not the last word. The return of Christ will bring about the defeat of death (1 Cor. 15:54–55). Reflecting and writing on the subject of resurrection hope has been personally edifying, and it is a privilege to contribute to the Short Studies in Biblical Theology. I am grateful to Crossway and to the series editors, Dane Ortlund and Miles Van Pelt, for the opportunity. I admire these men, and their encouragement has been a blessing.

My wife Stacie read an early draft of this manuscript, and her feedback and discerning pen instantly improved these chapters. How she set aside time to do this amid schooling and caring for our four boys, I'll never know! I'm grateful that my friends Jonathan Ketcham, Patrick Schreiner, and Samuel Bierig read the manuscript and shared helpful feedback and recommendations that strengthened it. Chris Cowan, my Crossway editor, was great to work with, and his keen eye and skills were a blessing to receive.

The topic of resurrection hope is dear to my heart. I wrote on it for my doctoral work at the Southern Baptist Theological Seminary, and I've enjoyed writing and preaching on it over the years. Our hope as Christians is great because the Savior we love is great, and our hope in him is sure because he himself is faithful.

I've dedicated *Resurrection Hope and the Death of Death* to Andrew Peterson. I learned about his music nearly twenty years ago, and his albums have meant more to me and our family with each passing year. The songs from his heart are full of hope, and many of his lyrics exult in the power of God over sin and corruption and death. Whether you are listening to his *Resurrection Letters* and *Behold the Lamb of God* albums or reading his Wingfeather Saga books, you are hearing about the power of faith, hope, and love. He writes and sings to light up the dark. Thank you, Andrew, for all that you have offered to the world. Your music and books have made it a better place. Given the reality of the risen Jesus, Paul writes, "Be steadfast, immovable, always abounding in the work of the Lord, knowing that in the Lord your labor is not in vain" (1 Cor. 15:58).

Introduction

What kind of life were you made for? Before you answer that question, here's another: what was life like before the rebellion of our first parents? The state of their existence provides a clue, a pointer, to answering the first question.

Embodied life. Adam and Eve experienced life and God's good creation with bodies. From the beginning it was this way. They didn't exist before their bodies. And this pattern is affirmed and vindicated at the end of Holy Scripture, when death is done because the dead have been raised.

Death the Disrupter

Looking at the beginning and the end of divine revelation, we can see that an embodied life is good, desirable, and coming. Death is the disrupter. For now, we experience embodied life temporarily because the effects of sin and the curse will not permit unending life. Outside Eden, we outwardly waste away. Our breath of life will, at some near or distant moment, cease.

Yet the biblical authors essentially say to death, "You shall surely die." Those wrapped in death's cords will be raised, and the saints will dwell in immortal bodies to experience the life they were made for, an existence surpassing even the glories of the garden. We might consider this world to be the land of the living, but the reality is more complicated than that. We can just as well consider this world to be the land of the dying. We're breathing now in the valley of the shadow of death. Under the sun nothing lasts, not even us.

Risen Hope

The sinner's only hope in life and death is Jesus Christ—a hope that is grounded in his victorious person and work. He is the Savior of sinners because he lives and reigns. He has broken the cords of death, and he lives as the firstfruits of the life that will be fully ours. For Jesus, the valley of death's shadow led to vindication and exaltation, and that is the path we walk.

The good news about Jesus includes his virginal conception, his sinless life, and his sin-bearing death, but the gospel is incomplete without the empty tomb. If Jesus remained defeated by death, his perpetual entombment would call into question everything he said and did before the cross. The resurrection of Jesus on the third day is crucial to the good news, and the good news is emptied of its power without it. Paul says that if Jesus hasn't been raised, then we're still in our sins, our preaching is powerless, and our hope is in vain (1 Cor. 15:12–19).

When Jesus rose from the dead, the perishable put on the imperishable; and because he did, we will. Our hope is risen, so our hope is sure. He died never to die again.

The Biblical Landscape

Jesus's resurrection is announced in the New Testament, but the hope for resurrection is older than the empty tomb. To consider such a vibrant topic as resurrection hope, we will need the whole Bible. All its genres will help us. Many biblical authors will weigh in as we construct a vision of how resurrection hope unfolds across the sweep of Scripture.

When you think of resurrection hope, you might naturally turn to the New Testament. And that's understandable, because that hope is loud and lively there. But the volume was getting loud already in the Old Testament, and we will begin there.

The Old Testament of Jesus's day was divided into three parts: the Law, the Prophets, and the Writings. This book will treat each part in chapters 1–3. Then chapters 4–7 will investigate the New Testament, treating the Gospels, Acts, the Letters, and Revelation. The biblical landscape is vast, but that's appropriate to the vast nature of resurrection hope.

Resurrection Sightings

The resurrection of Jesus, and the hope for our own liberation from death, is foretold and foreshadowed in the Old Testament. The prophet Daniel says that people will rise from death, some to everlasting life and others to everlasting judgment (Dan. 12:2). The prophet Ezekiel depicts the exile and return of the Israelites as a corporate death and resurrection (Ezek. 37). Jonah descends into the depths in a fish before ascending to the shore after three days (Jonah 2; cf. Matt. 12:40).

The psalm writers sing about being brought out of the pit, about being taken from the clutches of death. They herald their hope to see God and to stand before him. These songs are from the lips of those who live in the land of the dying, and they write with their gazes fixed on the future land of the living. The suffering and sorrowful psalmists write as if death is not the end and something greater than earthly life is on the way.

Pushing deeper into Old Testament history, we remember that the Lord used both Elijah and Elisha to deliver people from death (1 Kings 17; 2 Kings 4). These are historical narratives where the power of death faced the power of God. And let's not forget that

Elijah himself ascended to God without dying first (2 Kings 2). A whirlwind of fire carried him above the earth, and suddenly—as with Enoch many generations earlier—death didn't seem so inevitable.

Even individuals who had not witnessed a physical resurrection could still hold out hope that God's power was greater than death. Two thousand years before Jesus was born, Abraham and Isaac left their traveling companions and climbed a mountain for sacrifice (Gen. 22). Abraham told them that he and the boy were going to worship and would return. The aging patriarch knew he could trust God, that God would keep his promise of bringing offspring through Isaac even though Isaac had not yet fathered a child (21:12). If God's plan was for Abraham to offer Isaac, then God's plan must also be to raise Isaac from the dead. Abraham's resurrection faith was reasonable because he knew from experience that God is serious about promises and has the power to bring them to pass (21:1–2).

An Everlasting Remedy

The Old and New Testaments testify that the solution to the problem of death is resurrection. The storyline of Scripture takes us from the embodied first couple in Genesis to the glorified saints in the new creation. But we do not raise ourselves. The victor over death is the one who has command of death. The tombs will open when he says so (John 5:28–29).

In the Old Testament, no one experienced an immortal existence. What Jesus accomplished through his resurrection was something new, as well as a kind of life that earlier biblical authors only anticipated. The accounts of resurrections were stories of people brought back to earthly life only to die at a later date. Stepping out of the empty tomb on the third day, Jesus embodied the everlasting remedy to the problem of death: glorified immortality.

While the first Adam did not exist as a glorified image bearer, the last Adam does. We may be image-bearers who are born in Adam, but we will be raised in Christ because we are alive in Christ by faith already. Because he lives, we live and will live.

Why Resurrection Hope Matters

There are many worthy books to read and worthy topics to consider. Why should you read about resurrection hope? Here are five reasons.

1. *Individual*: you are going to die. I know this isn't news to you, but you might not ponder it often enough. Resurrection hope affords you the opportunity to think about death clearly and without delusion. You are not invincible. As you age, you will face the aches and afflictions associated with getting older in a fallen world. And since you are going to die, shouldn't you have a clear understanding of your hope in the face of death?

2. *Relational*: people you know are going to die. You may even be at their bedside when it happens. You will know people who die old and others who die young. The healthy and the sick will die. The wise and the fool will die. All in all, we should count it a great privilege to point others to truth and hope in Christ. And resurrection hope is part of what we should share. The more we know about it, the more sound and helpful our instruction will be.

3. *Christological*: Jesus has been raised from the dead. He is the object of our faith and hope, so we must commit ourselves to learn about what he has accomplished. His victorious resurrection and glorified body are not bonus facts for an otherwise solid faith. If you negate the resurrection hope that Jesus embodies and promises, there is no gospel worth preserving or preaching.

4. *Theological*: resurrection hope intersects with other biblical doctrines. In thinking about resurrection hope, we must think about—for example—the goodness of creation, the nature of man,

the problem of sin, and the final state of all things. As we strive to understand the Bible and to hold together its many teachings, a study of resurrection hope will prove necessary and profitable.

5. *Doxological*: the hope of resurrection should stir joy and praise to God. The promise of resurrection extols the power of God and showcases the faithfulness of God, all to the glory of his name. Since Christians want to be those whose hearts are aflame with worship, we should delight in whatever stokes and feeds that flame. Gaining greater clarity about resurrection hope will help us exalt the Lord with greater zeal and joy.

1

Resurrection Hope in the Law

The roots of resurrection hope run deep. Long before prophets like Isaiah and Daniel shouted the news of future life over death, the seeds of this hope were growing in fertile soil. This chapter will explore ways in which the Law—Genesis through Deuteronomy—stimulates and lays the foundation for resurrection hope.[1]

As we walk through the Law, or the Torah, we will begin in the garden of Eden. Then we will go through the flood and into the lives of the patriarchs. We will follow the Israelites to Egypt and then leave with them through the mighty exodus. The redeemed people must live set apart to their holy God, so we will behold how the God of life dwells with sinners. They can count on his power and faithfulness, and these characteristics—divine power and faithfulness—are central to the hope that death will die.

---

1. Some scholars are reluctant to find instances of resurrection hope earlier than Dan. 12:2 (or perhaps Isa. 26:19). T. D. Alexander summarizes critical scholarship on the subject: "It is not uncommon to encounter statements which suggest that the Old Testament has almost nothing to say on the subject of life after death; and what little it does report is usually assessed in quite negative terms" ("The Old Testament View of Life After Death," *Themelios* 11, no. 2 [1986]: 41).

Take and Eat and Live Forever

In the beginning, God made embodied image bearers. From the ground he made Adam, and from Adam he made Eve (Gen. 2:7, 21–22). This first couple didn't exist before their physical forms. God breathed life into their bodies, and these bodies—like everything else God had made—were good (1:31).[2]

Adam and Eve lived in the abundance of God's blessing. Sources of food were plentiful, and the couple could fulfill the divine commission to be fruitful, multiply, and exercise dominion over God's creation (1:28). They would be God's viceregents, representing the King of creation as his agents, his royal ambassadors. Their physical bodies were integral to how they would rule and fulfill their commission.

But the bodies of God's image bearers were not immortal. He had warned Adam about eating from the forbidden tree: "In the day that you eat of it you shall surely die" (2:17). In those words, the notion of death occurs for the first time in Scripture. God is the God of life, and his ways are the ways of life; therefore, to reject God and his ways is to embrace death.

Another special tree was in the garden of Eden: the tree of life (2:9). This tree represented more than sustenance. The fruit of this tree enabled one to live forever. We know this because of God's words when he expelled the rebellious image bearers from Eden: "lest he reach out his hand and take also of the tree of life and eat, and live forever" (3:22). Adam and Eve left the garden in their perishable bodies, and they would experience what God promised:

---

2. According to Kelly Kapic, "Unlike Plato's philosophy, the biblical presentation frames original human goodness within bodily existence, not apart from it. Our physicality was not a problem to be overcome but a gift essential to our existence. . . . Put differently, communion with God and others was always meant to take place in and through the body, not apart from it. This was our created state; this will be our ultimate hope" (*Embodied Hope: A Theological Meditation on Pain and Suffering* [Downers Grove, IL: IVP Academic, 2017], 46).

> for you are dust,
>> and to dust you shall return. (3:19)

The tree of life held out the hope of physical immortality, which was something Adam and Eve didn't have but were made for.[3] The problem of sin corrupts God's good design, so they died outside of Eden. Barred from access to that tree, their bodies eventually returned to the dust. The question for sinners, then, is this: will the perishable ever put on imperishable, so that the hope of immortal bodily life might be attained after all?

In the fullness of God's Word, resurrection life is how sinners will experience the fruit from that Edenic tree. The hope of immortal bodily life was not lost forever.[4]

The Forces of Death

When you think of death, do you think exclusively about the stopping of the heart and breath? The ending of breath and heartbeats is most surely death, but in the Bible death is more than this. The forces of death are visible and active in this fallen world.

We should allow the Bible's depictions of death to influence how we think about the problem of death in this world. Interpreters may not see how resurrection hope is present in some passages if they haven't noticed how death is present in other passages.

The outworking of death takes manifold forms. Whatever inhibits, harms, or destroys life is a kind of death.[5] When the biblical

---

3. Bruce Waltke says, "This highest potency of life was available in the garden and . . . will be experienced consummately in the resurrection of our bodies" (*An Old Testament Theology: An Exegetical, Canonical, and Thematic Approach* [Grand Rapids, MI: Zondervan, 2007], 257).

4. L. Michael Morales writes, "The end of redemption is not to live a bodiless, ethereal existence in the afterlife of heaven but rather to be raised up in glory with a real, new-creation body for a life of unending joy with God the Father, Son, and Holy Spirit" (*Exodus Old and New: A Biblical Theology of Redemption* [Downers Grove, IL: IVP Academic, 2020], 3).

5. Morales says, "The path of exile through Eden's gates was, therefore, a path from life to death, from light to darkness, from harmony to dysfunction and strife, from health to sickness,

authors tell of God's power that restores, frees, heals, or raises, you are reading about the power of life overcoming the forces of death.[6] The reason resurrection hope is more prevalent in Scripture than it may first seem is because the promises and actions of the God of life pervade the testimony of the biblical authors.

Death through Exile

Although God warned that eating from the forbidden tree would bring death (Gen. 2:17), Adam and Eve did not immediately die physically. But their disobedience corrupted their relationship with God (3:7–13). Sin brought alienation and shame. The blessings of marriage and childbearing would be affected (3:16), and the privilege of labor and vocation would be affected as well (3:17–19).

We shouldn't read God's warning in Genesis 2:17 as a threat unfulfilled. Adam and Eve sinned and fell short of the glory of God. There is more to dying than physical death. Eden was the realm of God's presence and bountiful provision; it was the realm of life. Exile from Eden meant separation from where God had placed them. Since God barred reentry to the garden and access to the tree of life, their exile was a kind of death. The separation from sacred space meant a move away from life.[7]

---

from security to violence, from compassion to inhumanity, from wholeness to brokenness, from peace with God to enmity—from a life of friendship with God to alienation" (*Exodus Old and New*, 9).

6. Jon Levenson explains, "Death and life in the Hebrew Bible are often best seen as relational events and are for the selfsame reason inseparable from the personal circumstances of those described as living or as dead. To be alive in this frequent biblical sense of the word inevitably entailed more than merely existing in a certain physical state. It also entailed having one's being within a flourishing and continuing kin group that dwelt in a productive and secure association with its land. Conversely, to be widowed, bereaved of children, or in exile was necessarily to experience death. Indeed, each of these states (even death) and others (notably, health or illness) could serve as a synecdoche for the condition brought about by any of the others" (*Resurrection and the Restoration of Israel: The Ultimate Victory of the God of Life* [New Haven, CT: Yale University Press, 2006], 154–55).

7. This concept would be applied later to the tabernacle in the middle of Israel's encampment and also to the nation of Israel going into Babylonian captivity during their exile.

When we see a reversal of this direction, when a figure moves from the realm of death into sacred space, we are watching the power of life at work. The exile of Adam—and thus of all people—from sacred space leads to this question: will the God of life bring his people out of the realm of the dead? Returning from exile, moving from death to life, would be resurrection.[8]

The Taking of Enoch

Outside Eden, the generations die. The widespread reality of death is clear in the genealogy of Genesis 5. The rhythm of death is in verse after verse. The pattern consists of a person's name, a descendant, the total years of life, and then the report that "he died." The repetition builds such an expectation of death that the words about Enoch jolt the reader: "Enoch walked with God, and he was not, for God took him" (Gen. 5:24).

The taking of Enoch did not involve death. Since the onset of human death in a post-Genesis-3 world, every person had died. Then suddenly and mysteriously, Enoch was taken after walking with God for hundreds of years. Enoch did not return to the dust from which he had come. Instead, God delivered him from death. This rapturous report is a light of hope against the dark backdrop of the dead.

If God could deliver someone *before* death, could he deliver someone *after* death? If the God of life could disrupt the rhythm of death that permeated the generations in Genesis 5, what else could he do? The example of Enoch isn't meant to provide any guarantee that the faithful will be delivered before earthly death, but his example does show that God is greater than death. Death wasn't so invincible after all. Its claim on sinners could be overruled.

---

8. According to Morales, "Separated from Yahweh God, the fountain of life and being, humanity's condition is one of death. As such, the return to God—the exodus—can only be life from the dead, deliverance from death" (*Exodus Old and New*, 7).

Decreation and Recreation of the Earth

The genealogy of Genesis 5 ends with the family of Noah (Gen. 5:32). And it is during the days of Noah that the effects of sin reach a horrific scale and scope. God announces judgment (6:13). The deluge on the earth in Genesis 6–7 is a watery death for creation, yet creation emerges from judgment in Genesis 8.

The words *decreation* and *recreation* can be used to interpret God's judgment in light of the imagery in Genesis 1. God brought land from the waters and then later filled that land with animals and people (1:9–10, 24–31). When God covered people, animals, and land with the floodwaters, the reader is to picture a decreation.

God remembered Noah and the ark's other occupants (8:1). His wind blew over the earth, and the waters subsided.[9] Land appeared once more, and the ark emptied to fill the land. God brought life through death, deliverance through judgment.

The association of the deluge with death and resurrection is confirmed by later Scripture. Peter says baptism corresponds to the deliverance of people through the waters of judgment (1 Pet. 3:20–21). Baptism is a new covenant ordinance that pictures death to sin and new life in Christ (Rom. 6:3–4). In union with the redeeming King, we have come alive out of the deadness of our trespasses (Eph. 2:4–6).

The imagery of recreation in Genesis 8 does not suggest a return to a pre-fall state. But the episode of the deluge does confirm for readers that God is serious about sin, he is a righteous Judge, and the wicked will not endure forever in their rebellion. The return of Christ will mean a new heavens and new earth (2 Pet. 3:8–13; Rev. 21:1–5). Making all things new will be, on a cosmic scale, resurrecting creation to a glorified and everlasting state.

---

9. The word *wind* in Gen. 8:1 can be translated "Spirit." Language about the Spirit over the waters is another link to creation (see 1:2).

The Barren Womb

Moving from the global canvas of the great deluge, let's focus on the individual obstacle of childlessness. The multiplying of generations meant the advance of life, but a barren womb meant the death of the family line.[10] When Rachel said to her husband Jacob, "Give me children, or I shall die!" (Gen. 30:1), her statement was more than a cry of desperation. Before Jacob and Rachel, Isaac and Rebekah faced barrenness (25:21). And before Isaac and Rebekah, Abraham was married to Sarah who was barren (11:30).

The biblical author highlights the reality of barrenness in the wives of the patriarchs in order to exalt the power of God that overcomes even this obstacle. God brings life to the dead womb. Abraham and Sarah conceive, as do Isaac and Rebekah, as do Jacob and Rachel. Conception for a barren womb is the triumph of life over death.[11] Not only is the woman no longer barren, the vitality of the family line continues through the descendant that will be born.

When Sarah conceives in Genesis 21, the biblical author emphasizes God's power: "the LORD did to Sarah as he had promised" (21:1). Pressed together in this verse is the notion of God's power (what the Lord "did") and the notion of God's promise ("as he had promised"). God once asked Abraham, "Is anything too hard for the LORD?" (18:14). That question is key to the whole discussion of resurrection. Death is strong; the grave seems so inevitable and invincible. Our days are numbered. But God is the God of life, and he has the ability to fulfill what he has promised.

---

10. Levenson says, "Given the construction of personal identity in the Hebrew Bible, infertility and the loss of children serve as the functional equivalent of death. Striking at each generation of the patriarchs of Genesis, and then at Judah in the next, childlessness in one or both of these modes threatens to terminate the family, thus evoking the terror that later generations (including our own) feel in the face of their personal deaths" (*Resurrection and the Restoration of Israel*, 119–20).

11. See Stephen G. Dempster, "From Slight Peg to Cornerstone to Capstone: The Resurrection of Christ on 'The Third Day' According to the Scriptures," *Westminster Theological Journal* 76 (2014): 386–87.

The Deliverance of Isaac

God had told Abraham that his offspring would come "through Isaac" (Gen. 21:12), but before Isaac had any descendants, God told Abraham to offer Isaac as a sacrifice on a mountain (22:2). Abraham journeyed in obedience, taking his son and some men with him. Arriving at the place, Abraham told the men, "Stay here with the donkey; I and the boy will go over there and worship and come again to you" (22:5).

Abraham's words evidence a resurrection faith. He used plural verbs for going, worshiping, and returning. He wasn't misleading the men lest they stop him from taking Isaac. He knew God had said to offer Isaac, yet he also knew that God had promised descendants through Isaac. If Isaac was going to be killed on the mountain, he was also going to be raised on the mountain. At the last moment before the sacrifice, the angel of the Lord told Abraham to stop (22:11–12). Isaac would be delivered. As the first installment of a larger pattern that will be established with later deliverances, Isaac is saved on the "third day" (22:4).

When the author of Hebrews reflects on the mountain experience of Genesis 22, he says that Abraham "considered that God was able even to raise him from the dead, from which, figuratively speaking, he did receive him back" (Heb. 11:19). Abraham believed God's promise, and he was confident in God's power. God would not tell Abraham to sacrifice Isaac unless God planned to raise Isaac so that offspring could come through him. Otherwise, God would be a promise breaker. Resurrection would prove God a promise keeper.

Surely part of Abraham's confidence in God's power was due to his own experience with Isaac's conception. God had brought life to a dead womb. Isaac was proof! And if God could bring life to a dead womb, he could bring life to a dead boy. One thing Abraham knew for certain was that God wouldn't break the divine promise of offspring through Isaac. He and Isaac would walk up the mountain together, and they would walk down the mountain too.

As Hebrews 11:19 alludes to the near-sacrifice of Isaac, the author says that Abraham received his son back from the dead "figuratively speaking." This language confirms that the threat and imminence of death is a real manifestation of the forces of death in this world.[12] A figurative resurrection took place on one of the mountains in Moriah. Even though Isaac did not physically die on the mountain, he was delivered from death nevertheless. And deliverance from death is resurrection.

The Rise of Joseph

Readers can discern a figurative resurrection in the story of Joseph. His life is an arc of descent and ascent. Joseph's brothers were ready to abandon him in a pit until the option of selling him to traders surfaced (Gen. 37:19–20, 26–28). While he served in an Egyptian household, Joseph's restraint and godliness provoked accusations of misconduct (39:7–19), and his master placed him in prison (39:20). The pit and the prison represent Joseph's descent. But wherever Joseph was and whatever Joseph did, God was with him (39:21–23).

The rise of Joseph began in prison. Pharaoh became aware of Joseph's ability to interpret dreams, and Joseph aided the Egyptian king (41:1–36). As a result, Pharaoh wanted Joseph to serve in his administration. Joseph became head of all Egypt, second only to Pharaoh himself (41:40–44).

---

12. Byron Wheaton says that Hebrews 11:19 "provides us with several clues for reading other narratives of the OT for their allusion to the resurrection. First, the 'victim' is under some sort of sentence of death. Second, the process of execution is in progress. Third, there is no human possibility of rescue; the end is imminent. Fourth, the dying process is miraculously overcome so that the victim is restored to life. Fifth, the 'resurrection' issues in a new future for the victim and those associated with him" ("As It Is Written: Old Testament Foundations for Jesus' Expectation of Resurrection," *Westminster Theological Journal* 70 [2008]: 248).

God vindicated Joseph out of the forces of oppression and servitude. Figuratively speaking (see Heb. 11:19), God raised Joseph from the dead. And his vindication brought blessing and life to others. His brothers came to Egypt needing food, and he provided for them. When Jacob's whole family relocated from Canaan to the land of Goshen, Joseph saw to their flourishing (Gen. 46–47). The rise of Joseph meant life and blessing for everyone united to him.

Burying Bones in Canaan

Though the end of Genesis tells of the Israelites dwelling in a foreign land, the story is unfinished. God had promised that Abraham and his descendants would inherit the land of Canaan (Gen. 12:7; 15:18–20; 17:8). God reiterated this promise to Isaac and to Jacob (26:3–5; 28:13–15). It is noteworthy, however, that these three patriarchs died before possessing the land. They died in faith, looking toward the fulfillment of God's promises.

The faith of the patriarchs is demonstrated by their burial decisions. Abraham was buried in the cave of Machpelah, which he had purchased in Canaan for Sarah's burial years earlier (25:9–10). Isaac was buried in the same place, and Jacob asked to be buried there as well (49:29–31). At the end of Genesis, as Joseph neared death, he told his brothers, "God will surely visit you, and you shall carry up my bones from here" (50:25). That request confirms that Joseph wanted his bones buried in Canaan too (see Josh. 24:32).

The desire for burial in Canaan signaled a faith in God's promise that they would inherit the land as an everlasting possession. If they hadn't received the land before they died, they believed they would receive it in the future. The bones in the cave at Machpelah would be raised. Resurrection from the dead would be the way these patriarchs could receive all that God had promised them. They died in faith and would rise in glory. They died as heirs and would rise as possessors.

They wanted their bones buried in Canaan because death, somehow, would not prevent God's promises from coming to pass. Is anything too hard for the Lord?

The Rescue of Baby Moses

If resurrection can be pictured by deliverance from imminent threat and death, then the rescue of baby Moses qualifies as an example of this. The Nile River was to receive all the newborn Hebrew males unto death (Ex. 1:22). But Moses's mother placed him in a basket, a little ark, and she put it by the riverbank (2:3).[13] Like Noah's large ark that kept those inside from the watery death (Gen. 6–7), this small basket protected baby Moses from watery death.[14]

The rescue of Moses led to his incorporation into Pharaoh's household (Ex. 2:10). Decades after fleeing Egypt for Midian as an adult (2:15), Moses encountered the Lord on Mount Sinai (3:1–6). The one who had been rescued would become the rescuer. God said, "Come, I will send you to Pharaoh that you may bring my people, the children of Israel, out of Egypt" (3:10).

The Exodus of the Israelites

The land of Goshen was filled with Israelites, but that land wasn't the one promised to Abraham, Isaac, and Jacob. The right people were in the wrong place. Egyptian leaders had become oppressors. A new pharaoh wanted the Israelites enslaved in bitter and hard service (Ex. 1:8–14). Lives of flourishing became lives of hardship and subjection. The Israelites were the corporate son of God (4:22), and God's son needed deliverance.

---

13. The "ark" in Gen. 6:14 is the same word as the "basket" in Ex. 2:3.

14. Wheaton comments on Moses's name, which is mentioned in Ex. 2:10 after the servant girl raised him from the riverbank: "His name attests to his being delivered/resurrected from the waters" ("As It Is Written," 250). "Moses" sounds like the Hebrew word for "draw out."

The exodus of the Israelites occurred against the backdrop of the death of the firstborn sons in Egypt during the tenth and final plague (12:29–30). With the cries of their captors hanging in the air, the Israelites emerged from their captivity and left under the leadership of Moses. As Morales explains, "The exodus pattern is nothing less than the reversal of exile, nothing less than resurrection from the dead."[15]

From the corporate death of slavery, the Israelites rose to embrace their heaven-wrought liberation. They had been exiles in the foreign land of Egypt, but now they were pressing toward the land of promise. Their return to Canaan, hundreds of years after they left it through their ancestor Jacob, was a corporate resurrection. The God of life had been mightily at work and now would lead them with cloud and fire. Liberation from Egypt is a picture of future life from the dead, for "resurrection is the ultimate and final liberation."[16]

With the Egyptians pursuing the Israelites, Moses led them as he followed the cloud of God, and they came to the shore of the Red Sea. Despite the fearful and faltering Israelites, Moses followed the Lord's instructions and stretched out his hand over the sea, so that the waters divided (Ex. 14:21). The waters, which could have been Israel's destruction, stood as walls on their right and left as they passed through to the other side on dry ground (14:29).

God thus brought them through death, consummating their deliverance which would reverberate through future songs and prophecies for generations.[17]

---

15. Morales, *Exodus Old and New*, 16.

16. Levenson, *Resurrection and the Restoration of Israel*, 28.

17. Morales says, "Even Israel's historical exodus out of Egypt is portrayed as a symbolic resurrection through the waters of death, out of Egypt as a figurative Sheol inhabited by the sea dragon, Pharaoh. The return of Jews from exile too is likened to a resurrection out of death and the grave, a prophesied second exodus. Time and again the concepts of exodus and resurrection are united deeply" (*Exodus Old and New*, 185).

The Tabernacle within the Camp

After their deliverance through the Red Sea, the Israelites journeyed to Mount Sinai. And there the Lord made known, through Moses, the instructions about his portable dwelling place. The people constructed this tabernacle, and it would go with them as they traveled.

The encampment of the Israelites had several realms, and their progression is noteworthy. While traveling from Mount Sinai to the promised land, the Israelites camped around the tabernacle (Ex. 40; Num. 2). The tabernacle—or tent of meeting—represented the life and glory of God dwelling in the midst of his redeemed people.

To approach the tabernacle for offerings at the sacrificial altar, the Israelites needed to be "clean," or ritually fit. Only the priests could enter the large room, the Holy Place. And only the high priest, once a year on the Day of Atonement, had access to the cube-shaped room behind the veil known as the Most Holy Place (Lev. 16). There, the glory of God was manifest over the lid of the golden ark (Ex. 25:10–22).

A move away from the tabernacle was movement away from life. Beyond the tabernacle courtyard was the encampment of the Israelites. Those who were unclean could not approach the tabernacle until their uncleanness was resolved and they were once more fit for ritual acts. Those who were perpetually unclean had to dwell outside the Israelite camp. Outside the camp was the realm of exile, far from the life of God and the community of God's people. Exile was like death. And ritual uncleanness was a move toward the direction of death. Restoration to the status of clean was a move toward life.

Viewed as a whole, the tabernacle, the encampment, and the area beyond the camp are realms reminiscent of the garden of Eden, Eden itself, and the land beyond Eden. Exile was a move toward death. Entering the tabernacle courtyard, and entering the tabernacle itself through priestly representatives, was entering the realm of life. With God dwelling in the midst of his people, the power of life had come to push back against impurity and uncleanness and against the forces of death.

Unresolved Skin Disease

Any skin disease rendered someone ritually unfit to approach the tabernacle, but an unresolved skin disease meant that the afflicted person had to dwell outside the camp. God told Moses,

> The leprous person who has the disease shall wear torn clothes and let the hair of his head hang loose, and he shall cover his upper lip and cry out, "Unclean, unclean." He shall remain unclean as long as he has the disease. He is unclean. He shall live alone. His dwelling shall be outside the camp. (Lev. 13:45–46)

The exiled state of the perpetually diseased person signals unfitness for the realm of life. Lepers were the walking dead. Their clothes and hair were disheveled, and they dwelled outside the camp. A leper's physical appearance was like a person outwardly wasting away.

Should a leper be healed, the power of life has conquered the forces of death at work on the body. The restoration of disease-ridden skin means vitality and flourishing, the return to community and family and—most importantly—tabernacle worship. If lepers are like the walking dead, then a healed leper has conquered death.

Dying and Rising in the Wilderness

Bearing the tabernacle and the regulations to approach it, the Israelites continued their trek to the promised land by crossing the wilderness. But the Israel that emerged from the wilderness at the end of Numbers was not the same Israel that entered it. The older generation of Israelites had, by and large, rebelled against Moses and declared their desire for Egypt (Num. 14:1–4). For forty years the Israelites wandered in the wilderness until the last of that generation died, as judgment from the Lord (14:33–35).

The children of the wilderness generation grew up during those forty years, and they were the new Israel to cross the Jordan River and inherit the promised land. During the wilderness decades, then, some Israelites would fall while others would rise. The rebels against Moses had been purged through death, and rising in their place was the group who would follow Joshua's lead into Canaan.

Raising Up a Prophet Like Moses

Before Moses died and Joshua led the people to their inheritance, a word about the future was necessary. The prophet Moses told the Israelites that God would bring a mighty prophet into the midst of his people sometime in the future: "The Lord your God will raise up for you a prophet like me from among you, from your brothers—it is to him you shall listen" (Deut. 18:15). God said of this future figure, "I will put my words in his mouth, and he shall speak to them all that I command him. And whoever will not listen to my words that he shall speak in my name, I myself will require it of him" (18:18–19).

It is possible that God's promise to "raise up" a prophet like Moses meant only to bring such a figure onto the stage of history, but more may be intended. The promise to "raise up" sounds like resurrection. Will this future figure come not only into human history but up from the grave itself? Will this future figure, whose mouth speaks God's words, be vindicated with authority in a way that far surpasses the prophet Moses? In the book of Acts, Peter interprets Deuteronomy 18 this way. In Acts 3:22, Peter cites Moses's words about the Lord raising up a prophet. And in 3:26, Peter says, "God, having raised up his servant, sent him to you first, to bless you by turning every one of you from your wickedness."

In the context of Peter's words in Acts 3, the resurrection of Jesus is in view. There were people who "killed the Author of life, whom God raised from the dead" (Acts 3:15). God had told Moses that a future prophet would be raised up, and Peter pronounced the fulfillment of that prophecy. God had raised up Jesus from death.

The God Who Makes Alive

Near the end of Deuteronomy, Moses recites the words of a song in the hearing of the Israelites. Included is this bold divine assertion:

> See now that I, even I, am he,
>> and there is no god beside me;
> I kill and I make alive;
>> I wound and I heal;
>> and there is none that can deliver out of my hand.
>> (Deut. 32:39)

To this point in the Torah narrative, there is no report of someone being raised physically from death. But there have been multiple instances of God's power bringing life and restoration. The forces of death are no match for the power of life. God asserts the ability to "kill" and "make alive," to "wound" and "heal." At first glance, perhaps the first pair of words is only a claim to have the ability to end the lives of the living. But that interpretation is insufficient.

The words in Moses's song are arranged with synonymous parallelism in Deuteronomy 32:39. The claim "I kill and I make alive" is parallel in the next line with "I wound and I heal." In the second pair, wounding and healing must refer to the same person and in that order. The one wounded is the one who needs healing. When we understand the second pair of terms this way, the meaning of the first pair becomes clearer. God asserts his power to end life ("I kill") and to restore life ("I make alive"), in that order and for the same person.[18] God himself claims the power to raise the dead.[19]

A Word from Paul

Fifteen hundred years after Moses's song, the apostle Paul stood before Felix at Caesarea. And in that trial setting, Paul made a statement that we need to incorporate into our exploration of the Law. Some Jews were charging Paul with instigating riots and trying to profane the temple (Acts 24:5–6). Paul's response included this claim:

> But this I confess to you, that according to the Way, which they call a sect, I worship the God of our fathers, believing everything laid down by the Law and written in the Prophets, having a hope in God, which these men themselves accept, that there will be a resurrection of both the just and the unjust (24:14–15).

Let's consider what Paul said. He believed in a coming resurrection, and both the just and the unjust—believers and unbelievers—will be raised from death. Why did Paul believe this? Because he believed what earlier Scripture teaches. Which part of Scripture?

---

18. Leila Bronner contends, "The arrangement of the key words . . . suggests that they are dealing with a resurrection motif" ("The Resurrection Motif in the Hebrew Bible: Allusions or Illusions?" *Jewish Bible Quarterly* 30, no. 3 [2002]: 145).

19. According to Leonard Greenspoon, "Since there is perhaps no other action of God's which displays the totality and uniqueness of His power more forcefully than the process by which He restores His dead to life, a reference to bodily resurrection is surely in keeping with the context at this point" ("The Origin of the Idea of Resurrection," in *Traditions in Transformation: Turning Points in Biblical Faith*, ed. Baruch Halpern and Jon D. Levenson [Winona Lake, IN: Eisenbrauns, 1981], 312).

He identified the Prophets but also the *Law*. Paul's belief in a future resurrection was rooted, ultimately, in the Pentateuch. While Paul did not identify which passages in the Pentateuch support the hope of God's power over the forces of death, the preceding sections of this chapter are examples of how to discern and affirm such a hope.

A Word from Jesus

While Paul believed both the Law and the Prophets were foundational for resurrection hope, the Sadducees held a different view. During the earthly ministry of Jesus, the Sadducees questioned him about resurrection. Their aim was to make resurrection seem absurd. They told a story about a childless couple. The man died and his widow married his brother, though still no offspring was born (Matt. 22:25). When that second man died, the woman married a third brother, and this pattern repeated through all seven brothers (22:26). The Sadducees asked, "In the resurrection, therefore, of the seven, whose wife will she be? For they all had her" (22:28).

The Sadducees affirmed only the Torah to be authoritative Scripture, and they didn't believe the Torah held out hope for a future resurrection. No doubt their confidence was strengthened by the fact that nowhere in the Torah is someone raised physically from the dead, nor is the word "resurrection" used anywhere from Genesis through Deuteronomy. But Jesus brought a strong word of correction: "You are wrong, because you know neither the Scriptures nor the power of God. For in the resurrection they neither marry nor are given in marriage, but are like angels in heaven" (Matt. 22:29–30).

Not only had the Sadducees misunderstood the nature of resurrection life (by supposing that earthly marriage was something that continued after the resurrection), but they also failed to understand the Scriptures and God's power.

If the Sadducees truly understood what the Torah teaches, they would have affirmed resurrection hope.[20] If they truly understood the reality and implications of God's power, they would have affirmed resurrection hope. Since the Sadducees affirmed the Torah, Jesus referred to it when he said, "And as for the resurrection of the dead, have you not read what was said to you by God: 'I am the God of Abraham, and the God of Isaac, and the God of Jacob'? He is not God of the dead, but of the living" (Matt. 22:31–32, citing Ex. 3:6).

It is common for scholars to interpret the statement "I am the God of Abraham, and the God of Isaac, and the God of Jacob" as meaning that the present-though-disembodied life of the patriarchs holds out hope for their resurrection as well.[21] This view may be correct, but perhaps the power of God is being invoked through the names Abraham, Isaac, and Jacob. These three patriarchs had all been married to barren women whose wombs experienced God's power enabling conception and life. The fictional story of the Sadducees was about marriages in which no offspring was conceived (Matt. 22:24–28), yet Jesus referred to real people for whom the power of life had overcome what was dead, in the families of Abraham, Isaac, and Jacob.[22]

Because the Sadducees didn't truly understand their Scriptures or the power of God, they couldn't discern God's lifegiving power over death.[23] When they read the Torah, resurrection hope wasn't clear.

---

20. Richard Hays explains, "Presumably, in fact, their rejection of the resurrection rests precisely on appeals to the authority of Scripture: no such belief was taught by Moses, so it should not be accepted. By challenging them at this point, Jesus creates the expectation that he will produce scriptural evidence to discredit their skepticism" ("Reading Scripture in Light of the Resurrection," in *The Art of Reading Scripture*, ed. Ellen F. Davis and Richard B. Hays [Grand Rapids, MI: Eerdmans, 2003], 226).

21. See, for example, Donald A. Hagner, *Matthew 14–28*, Word Biblical Commentary (Nashville: Thomas Nelson, 1995), 642; Leon Morris, *The Gospel according to Matthew*, Pillar New Testament Commentary (Grand Rapids, MI: Eerdmans, 1992), 561.

22. See this argument fleshed out in J. Gerald Janzen, "Resurrection and Hermeneutics: On Exodus 3.6 in Mark 12.26," *Journal for the Study of the New Testament* 23 (1985): 46–55.

23. Levenson says, "Levirate marriage is a mode of redemption of the dead" (*Resurrection and the Restoration of Israel*, 121).

When Jesus read the Torah, resurrection hope was obvious.[24] Bible readers and scholars should side with Jesus and not the Sadducees.

Conclusion

The God who called light to shine out of darkness can bring life to the dead. His power can conquer slavery and barrenness, prison and disease, exile and uncleanness, disaster and harm. The forces of death cannot resist the God of life. The Torah's narratives stir hope that the God of life will triumph over death not just partially but completely, not just temporally but forever. Through the glory of resurrection, we will feast on the fruit from the tree of life. Because of our union with Christ, the Last Adam, we will experience what we were made for: embodied immortality. Because God is faithful to his people and has the power to fulfill his promises, we can trust that death will surely die.

---

24. According to Richard Hays, Jesus "implies that knowledge of biblical content is not the same thing as 'knowing the Scriptures' in the way that matters. The telling of this controversy story suggests that authentic knowledge of the Scriptures depends on a hermeneutic of resurrection, the ability to discern in Scripture a witness of God's life-giving power" ("Reading Scripture in Light of the Resurrection," 226).

2

Resurrection Hope in the Prophets

God advances his promises and covenants in a world plagued by the forces of death. The second major section of the Old Testament is called the Prophets, and here the hope of resurrection becomes stronger and more explicit. These books take readers through the inheritance of the promised land, the darkness of the period when judges ruled, the rise of the monarchy in Jerusalem, and a multitude of prophets who proclaim a future vindication of the righteous and judgment on the wicked.

The Prophets consist of Joshua, Judges, 1–2 Samuel, 1–2 Kings, Isaiah, Jeremiah, Ezekiel, and the twelve Minor Prophets. The following examples from this literature will build on truths and expectations that were already established in the Torah. The God of life is active in his creation, displaying covenant faithfulness and divine power.

New Life in the Land

The Canaanites dwelled in idolatry and spiritual darkness, so the crossing of the Israelites over the Jordan River was the arrival of

God's life and light. By pillar and fire God had led them, and the ark of God went before them (Josh. 3:11). The conquest was God exercising dominion, through the Israelites, over the wicked.

Under Joshua's leadership, the Israelites inherited the promised land and experienced the faithfulness and power of God as he subdued their enemies (Josh. 6–12). Every broken high place was the darkness succumbing to light. Every ruined fortress and routed enemy was the forces of death being vanquished by life.

The book of Joshua tells the story of how the formerly enslaved nation received what God had promised to the patriarchs. The geographical movement from Egypt to Canaan is a move out of death and into life, from enslavement to inheritance.

The entrance of sacred space also recalls what was lost at the exile from Eden. The Israelites, like a new Adam, went into a sacred land that they might know, exult in, and live by the power of the lifegiving God who redeemed them and fought for them (Josh. 24:14–18).

The Cycle in Judges

After the conquest of the promised land and the death of Joshua, the Israelites experienced a spiritual decline. The book of Judges narrates a repeated cycle: the Israelites sin against the Lord, the Lord raises up an adversary, the people repent, and the Lord provides a judge who delivers the penitent people. This cycle covers the corporate demise and deliverance of the Israelites.

The biblical author says the Israelites provoked the Lord, and so "the anger of the Lord was kindled against Israel, and he gave them over to plunderers, who plundered them" (Judg. 2:14). Then the Lord "raised up judges, who saved them out of the hand of those who plundered them" (2:16). God raised up his people by raising up a judge (see 3:9). While sin brought the advance of death, God's power arrived with life and deliverance.

The Womb and Words of Hannah

During the period of the judges, there lived a woman named Hannah. She was barren, and so the family line through her was in jeopardy (1 Sam. 1:5). The Lord answered her prayer for a child, and she conceived and bore Samuel (1:20). God's power prevailed over the dead womb.

Hannah prayed to the Lord, and the content of her prayer includes a series of reversals. For example,

> The bows of the mighty are broken,
>> but the feeble bind on strength.
> Those who were full have hired themselves out for
>> bread,
> but those who were hungry have ceased to hunger.
>> (1 Sam. 2:4–5)

She also spoke in a way that called to mind her own reversal:

> The barren has borne seven,
>> but she who has many children is forlorn. (2:5)

Hannah had been barren and now had conceived. She continued to testify of God's power:

> The LORD kills and brings to life;
>> he brings down to Sheol and raises up. (2:6)

This claim recalls Deuteronomy 32:39, where God claimed to kill and make alive.

Hannah's words in 1 Samuel 2:6, like the earlier Torah reference, are about resurrection power.[1] Parallel to her words about the Lord

---

1. Leonard Greenspoon understands 1 Sam. 2:6 as "an expression of faith that death is not to be viewed as a permanent situation any more than earthly power or wealth. By His power to effect change, God can 'reverse the fortune' of those weak from the sleep of death through

ending life and restoring it is the statement about bringing someone down to Sheol and then back again. Scholars do not agree on
what Sheol means. It may be equivalent to the grave itself or to a
holding place beyond this earthly life.[2] Either way, the meaning
of Hannah's words is not lost. She extols God's power to raise
the dead.

Raising Up a Son for David

Years after Hannah gave birth to Samuel, he identified David as the
king from Judah's tribe who would rule over Israel (1 Sam. 16:12–13).
Through Nathan the prophet, King David learned of God's promise
about securing the throne. David had wanted to build a house for
God, but instead God would build a house—a dynasty—for David.
God said, "When your days are fulfilled and you lie down with your
fathers, I will raise up your offspring after you, who shall come from
your body, and I will establish his kingdom. He shall build a house
for my name, and I will establish the throne of his kingdom forever"
(2 Sam. 7:12–13).

One way to understand God's promise is that he would bring
an offspring from David's line onto the stage of history, and this
child—this son—would be the promised king who would rule forever. But there is an implication that must be addressed, because
human kings die. David died, Solomon died, Rehoboam died, and
so on. If God was going to keep the promise about a son reigning
forever on the Davidic throne, then this future king must overcome death. The Davidic throne would be established forever by
resurrection.

---

the introduction of the vitality of life" ("The Origin of the Idea of Resurrection," in *Traditions
in Transformation: Turning Points in Biblical Faith*, ed. Baruch Halpern and Jon D. Levenson
[Winona Lake, IN: Eisenbrauns, 1981], 314).

2. See Matthew Y. Emerson, *"He Descended to the Dead": An Evangelical Theology of Holy
Saturday* (Downers Grove, IL: IVP Academic, 2019).

When God promised, "I will raise up your offspring" (2 Sam. 7:12), the fulfillment would include not only the son's arrival but the raising up of the son after death. If death prevented kings from continuing in office, and if David's future son could overcome death, then that son could reign forever.

If we interpret 2 Samuel 7:12–13 as implying the future king's deliverance from death, that reading seems confirmed by Acts 13:22–23, 30–34, where Paul preached that God has fulfilled his promise to install the Christ by "raising Jesus" (Acts 13:33). Since the glorified Christ has defeated death, he has the necessary qualification to rule forever on the Davidic throne.

David Drawn Out of the Waters

The life of David contains episodes of threat and deliverance. In 2 Samuel 22, David sings of God's rescuing grace:

> He sent from on high, he took me;
>> he drew me out of many waters.
> He rescued me from my strong enemy,
>> from those who hated me,
>> for they were too mighty for me. (2 Sam. 22:17–18)

The imagery is reminiscent of Moses when he was drawn from the waters (Ex. 2:5–10). David depicts his deliverance from enemies as a deliverance from watery death. The upward motion is from death to life: God took David from the grip of many waters. David uses the imagery of death:

> For the waves of death encompassed me,
>> the torrents of destruction assailed me;
>> the cords of Sheol entangled me;
>> the snares of death confronted me. (2 Sam. 22:5–6)

David's enemies, whether Saul or Absalom or an entire army of foes, were like waves of death, and these waves were like the cords of Sheol. David's deliverance, therefore, was like resurrection.[3] If these cords were mightier than David, only someone who could overcome death would be able to help him.

Elijah and a Widow's Son

Under David's grandson Rehoboam, the kingdom of Israel divided (1 Kings 12:16–33). During these years of a fractured land, the Lord raised up prophets to bring the words and deeds of God to bear on the people.

In the ministry of Elijah, we see the first report of someone brought back from physical death. A widow's son died, and Elijah carried the dead body to the upper chamber of her home (17:17–19). After stretching himself on the child three times and crying out, "O Lord my God, let this child's life come into him again," the life of the child was restored (17:21–22).[4]

This miracle vindicates the biblical reasonableness that the God of covenant faithfulness and power could overcome physical death. God is sovereign over life and death, so Elijah prayed that God would restore the child's life. The prophet brought the son to his mother and said, "See, your son lives" (17:23).

The Taking of Elijah

As was the case with Enoch (Gen. 5:24), Elijah's earthly life did not end in death.[5] Elijah had walked with God and then was taken. He

---

3. According to Stephen Dempster, "David himself is a prime example of the defeat of the forces of death by the resurrecting power of God. It is as if death had wrapped its lethal tentacles around the king, and at the last moment Yahweh snatched him from their grasp" ("From Slight Peg to Cornerstone to Capstone: The Resurrection of Christ on 'The Third Day' According to the Scriptures," *Westminster Theological Journal* 76 [2014]: 394).

4. Greenspoon says, "In this context, what Elijah carried out could be termed a preliminary resurrection, but a resurrection nonetheless" ("The Origin of the Idea of Resurrection," 315).

5. As Derek Kidner put it, "At least twice the gates of Sheol had not prevailed" (*Genesis: An Introduction and Commentary*, Tyndale Old Testament Commentary [Downers Grove, IL: InterVarsity Press, 1967], 81).

"went up by a whirlwind into heaven" (2 Kings 2:11). God had stayed the jaws of death. Not only could God give life back to the dead (as in 1 Kings 17:21–22), but he could also prevent death from prevailing over someone.

The removal of Elijah was not broadly applied as a reward for everyone who walked faithfully with God. But the extraordinary sight of Elijah's ascension was a public declaration that death is not invincible, its appetite is not sovereign, and the God of life has the last word over his people. The future resurrection of the dead will be God's last word over the grave, and then death will be no more.

Elisha and the Shunammite's Son

Elisha was Elijah's successor, and like his predecessor, Elisha raised a dead person to life.[6] A Shunammite's son had died, and Elisha went to the room where he lay (2 Kings 4:32–33). He stretched out over the child, and the child opened his eyes (4:34–35). The young man inhaled the breath of life once more.

The young men raised from the dead by Elijah and Elisha were not raised in glorified bodies. Jesus was the firstfruits of glorified physicality (1 Cor. 15:20), which means these Old Testament resurrections were shadows of a greater resurrection to come. We don't know the names of the boys whom Elijah and Elisha brought back to life, but God knows. And their stories stir hope that the God of life who knows our names will fill us with everlasting breath.

---

6. Jon Levenson observes, "It is simply that long before the apocalyptic framework came into existence, the resurrection of the dead was thought possible—not according to nature, of course, but through the miraculous intervention of the living God" (*Resurrection and the Restoration of Israel: The Ultimate Victory of the God of Life* [New Haven, CT: Yale University Press, 2006], 132).

The Healing of Naaman

During the days of Elisha, a man named Naaman was healed of leprosy. When the reader learns of Naaman's affliction, the background of Leviticus 13–14 is important for interpretation. Naaman, though a Gentile, was a walking dead man. An Israelite girl who served in Naaman's household said, "Would that my lord were with the prophet who is in Samaria! He would cure him of his leprosy" (2 Kings 5:3). That prophet in view was Elisha. And the servant girl was right.

Elisha's instructions for Naaman were clear: "Go and wash in the Jordan seven times, and your flesh shall be restored, and you shall be clean" (5:10). Though initially reluctant, Naaman went to the Jordan River, dipped seven times in it, and "his flesh was restored like the flesh of a little child, and he was clean" (5:14). Since Naaman's skin disease demonstrated the forces of death at work in the world, his deliverance showcased the divine power of life.

The Bones of Elisha

The literature of 1–2 Kings tells of a third bodily deliverance from death. This story occurs after the death of Elisha but is still associated with him. "As a man was being buried, behold, a marauding band was seen and the man was thrown into the grave of Elisha, and as soon as the man touched the bones of Elisha, he revived and stood on his feet" (2 Kings 13:21).

The power of God was at work even through Elisha's bones. According to Greenspoon, "This account illustrates that Elisha's links with God as Divine Warrior were not severed by the prophet's death; rather, God continued to work through the prophet, even through his dead and buried bones, to bring about that reawakening to life which is resurrection."[7]

The Recovery of Hezekiah

King Hezekiah knew firsthand the power of the Divine Warrior when he experienced a personal resurrection of sorts. He had become sick "and was at the point of death" (2 Kings 20:1). He prayed, and the word of the Lord came to Isaiah for the king: "I have heard your prayer; I have seen your tears. Behold, I will heal you. On the third day you shall go up to the house of the LORD" (20:5).

Not only was Hezekiah delivered from death, but God delivered him on the third day. This third-day deliverance was a picture of resurrection. Hezekiah's illness was pulling him toward physical death; therefore, the act of divine intervention was the victory of life over death.

The Promise to Swallow Death

The prophet Isaiah ministered throughout the reign of King Hezekiah, and Isaiah's prophecies speak about resurrection hope on several occasions. In Isaiah 25, a vision foretells a day when death comes to an end. After describing a mountain of feasting and fellowship, the prophet says,

> And [God] will swallow up on this mountain
>> the covering that is cast over all peoples,
>> the veil that is spread over all nations.
> He will swallow up death forever;
>> and the Lord GOD will wipe away tears from all faces,

---

7. Greenspoon, "The Origin of the Idea of Resurrection," 306.

and the reproach of his people he will take away
from all the earth,
for the LORD has spoken. (Isa. 25:7–8)

The veil/covering over all peoples is death. But Isaiah says
that the day is coming when this veil will be removed. God will
swallow it, consume it. This consumption is death's destruction,
and death's destruction will be through the general resurrection.
The Lord will consume death by opening the tombs. This future
swallowing of death is what Paul has in mind when he writes
about resurrection hope: "When the perishable puts on the imperishable, and the mortal puts on immortality, then shall come to
pass the saying that is written: 'Death is swallowed up in victory'"
(1 Cor. 15:54).

Giving Birth to the Dead

One of the clearest statements of resurrection hope in the Old Testament is found in Isaiah 26:19:

Your dead shall live; their bodies shall rise.
You who dwell in the dust, awake and sing for joy!
For your dew is a dew of light,
and the earth will give birth to the dead.

The language is explicit about bodies rising, about those dwelling in
the dust waking up to sing.[8]

Dwelling in the dust is a metaphor for death, echoing Genesis 3:19:

for you are dust,
and to dust you shall return.

---

8. N. T. Wright calls Isa. 26:19 "the most obvious 'resurrection' passage in Isaiah" (*The Resurrection of the Son of God*, Christian Origins and the Question of God, vol. 3 [Minneapolis:
Fortress, 2003], 116).

Since giving birth is a picture of life, the earth's act of giving birth to the dead signals an act of resurrection: the dead come alive. Sometimes a biblical author will depict death as sleep from which one must awake, and that is the case in Isaiah 26:19. The dust-dwellers will wake up by resurrection. The sleep of death will be over.[9]

Blessing on People and Creation

In a world affected by sin and death, there are a myriad of conditions that need the blessing of God. Isaiah 35 presents a reversal of tragic conditions for the sake of flourishing, all due to God's blessing and power. At the beginning of the chapter, we read,

> The wilderness and the dry land shall be glad;
>> the desert shall rejoice and blossom like the crocus;
> it shall blossom abundantly
>> and rejoice with joy and singing. (Isa. 35:1–2)

The reversal will bring gladness to the wilderness and blossoming to the dry land.[10] The picture is Edenic. The barren land will be made fruitful. Later, in Isaiah 35,

> Then the eyes of the blind shall be opened,
>> and the ears of the deaf unstopped;
> then shall the lame man leap like a deer,
>> and the tongue of the mute sing for joy.
> For waters break forth in the wilderness,
>> and streams in the desert;

---

9. This is not equivalent to the notion of soul sleep. Rather, at death, the body is in the cords of the grave, at rest (or asleep) until resurrection.

10. According to Levenson, as the Divine Warrior "marches forth in wrath against the oppressive forces of chaos and death, nature languishes, and when he returns enthroned in victory and justice, nature flourishes and luxuriates" (*Resurrection and the Restoration of Israel*, 211).

> the burning sand shall become a pool,
>> and the thirsty ground springs of water;
> in the haunt of jackals, where they lie down,
>> the grass shall become reeds and rushes.
>> (Isa. 35:5–7)

Mixed with the imagery of creation being renewed is a variety of physical maladies being overcome: blindness, deafness, lameness, and muteness. This cluster of physical healings is the background to the kinds of miracles Jesus would perform in his earthly ministry. Physical restoration fuels the hope of resurrection.[11] After all, if the blind will see and the deaf will hear and the mute will speak and the lame will leap, what will the dead do?

The Prolonged Days of the Suffering Servant

Isaiah 53 is famous for its portrayal of the servant of the Lord bearing the iniquities of the sheep. This figure would be despised and rejected, stricken and afflicted, pierced and crushed (Isa. 53:3–5). He would be a lamb led to slaughter: taken away, cut off, and put into the grave (53:7–9). Jesus is the suffering servant of Isaiah 53, and he was flogged and crucified by Roman soldiers. But does this famous chapter, which foretells Christ's suffering and death, also anticipate a return to life?

The prophet writes,

> Yet it was the will of the LORD to crush him;
>> he has put him to grief;
> when his soul makes an offering for guilt,

---

11. Greenspoon says, "Man, as part of nature, could hardly remain unaffected. . . . The resurrection of man can be fit into the overall portrayal of nature's response to the victorious Divine Warrior" ("The Origin of the Idea of Resurrection," 276).

> he shall see his offspring; he shall prolong his days;
>
> the will of the LORD shall prosper in his hand. (53:10)

Though crushed and put to grief, the suffering servant will be vindicated. His days will be prolonged; he will see his offspring.[12] This atoning figure will die, but death is not the end. Vindication comes after death through resurrection.

Judgment on the Bodies of the Wicked

In the closing chapters of Isaiah's prophecy, the Lord speaks about the distant hope of new creation and judgment. There will be a new heavens and new earth, and people will worship the Lord (Isa. 66:22–23). The book of Revelation anticipates the fulfillment of this hope at Christ's return, when he will make all things new (Rev. 21:1).

In the final verse of Isaiah, following the language about new creation and worship, the Lord speaks about judgment on the bodies of the wicked. The righteous will know what happens to those who rebelled against God: "For their worm shall not die, their fire shall not be quenched, and they shall be an abhorrence to all flesh" (Isa. 66:24).[13] The portrayal is of unending physical abhorrence, the result of the just judgment of God who is sovereign over the righteous and the wicked. If the unrighteous have died and yet there is a future judgment for them that involves a physical state, then there will be a resurrection of the unrighteous for judgment.

---

12. G. K. Beale says this passage is "best read to refer to the Servant's recovery from death," thus resurrection (*A New Testament Biblical Theology: The Unfolding of the Old Testament in the New* [Grand Rapids, MI: Baker Academic, 2011], 232).

13. The word for "abhorrence" occurs twice in the Old Testament, here in Isa. 66:24 and in Dan. 12:2, indicating Daniel's dependence on Isa. 66:24 for the language about judgment on the resurrected bodies of the wicked.

The Bones That Come Alive

Like Isaiah, the prophet Ezekiel recorded prophecies about God's power over death. The prophecy in Ezekiel 37 is understandable against the background of corporate death and resurrection. Beginning in the book of Genesis, exile is a kind of death, and the return from exile is a kind of resurrection (Gen. 3:22–24). In Ezekiel's day, the Israelites were exiled into Babylonian captivity, and for decades they were displaced from the promised land while the apportioned judgment of God was completed.

But the Lord who dispersed them would regather them, hence the imagery in Ezekiel 37. The prophet has a vision of a valley of bones, and these bones are the people of Israel in their exiled state. The nation has died, becoming captive to wicked Babylon in a foreign land. Nevertheless, these bones will live. "Thus says the Lord GOD to these bones: Behold, I will cause breath to enter you, and you shall live. And I will lay sinews upon you, and will cause flesh to come upon you, and cover you with skin, and put breath in you, and you shall live, and you shall know that I am the LORD" (Ezek. 37:5–6).

In Ezekiel's vision, the bones assembled into bodies, and the bodies came to life by the power of God (37:10). God told him,

> Son of man, these bones are the whole house of Israel. Behold, they say, "Our bones are dried up, and our hope is lost; we are indeed cut off." Therefore prophesy, and say to them, Thus says the Lord GOD: Behold, I will open your graves and raise you from your graves, O my people. And I will bring you into the land of Israel. And you shall know that I am the LORD, when I open your graves, and raise you from your graves, O my people. (37:11–13)

Ezekiel was to tell the Israelites that they had a resurrection hope: God would bring them out of exile and into the promised land. The vision of Ezekiel makes sense if the foundation of resurrection hope has already been laid in earlier biblical revelation. God is faithful to his covenant promises, and he has the necessary power to fulfill those promises. Ezekiel's vision showcases the God of life whose power raises what had returned to the dust. This corporate hope is communicated with the imagery of individuals rising from the dead.

Without a prior hope of death's defeat, the power of the action in Ezekiel's vision is diminished.[14] The land of Babylon was the grave for Israel, yet Ezekiel's message is that God would call his people from the grave.

Raised Up on the Third Day

In the book of the Twelve, the prophet Hosea offers multiple examples of resurrection hope.[15] Chief among them is Hosea 6, where the disobedient Israelites voice language of repentance:

> Come, let us return to the LORD;
>
> > for he has torn us, that he may heal us;
>
> he has struck us down, and he will bind us up.
>
> After two days he will revive us;
>
> > on the third day he will raise us up,
>
> > that we may live before him. (Hos. 6:1–2)

---

14. As Greenspoon explains, "It is sufficiently clear that Ezekiel was working with a concept of the resurrection of the dead well enough known to his audience to allow for the simultaneous application of this belief to 'literal' resurrection and national restoration" ("The Origin of the Idea of Resurrection," 294).

15. In the Hebrew Bible, the twelve Minor Prophets are treated as a single book, the book of the Twelve.

Perhaps this expectation is informed by language from Deuteronomy 32:39, that the God who wounds can also heal, that the God who kills can also make alive again.

The people's words call for a return to Yahweh so that they can live before him. Sin brings judgment and death. Repentance is the way to life and restoration.[16] The Israelites want to be healed and bound, revived and raised up.[17] And they speak of being raised up on the third day. This "third day" detail is part of a pattern that readers can trace through other books, such as the deliverance of Isaac on the third day (Gen. 22:4) and the healing of Hezekiah on the third day (2 Kings 20:5).

If there wasn't already a concept that the God of life could overcome death, the power of the people's words would weaken. But since the biblical authors have already taught that God is mightier than the forces of death, the words of the Israelites are a reasonable hope and are coherent within the matrix of what earlier biblical writers have said.

The Promise to Redeem from Death

The Lord planned to judge the northern kingdom of Israel. An Assyrian army would conquer them. Still, the Israelites would not bear their guilt forever, for the God who struck them down would lift them up. God said,

> I shall ransom them from the power of Sheol;
> I shall redeem them from Death.

---

16. According to James Hamilton, "When he drives them from the land, they will enter the realm of the dead. They will die as a nation. Through the judgment of Yahweh's tearing like a lion comes the salvation of Yahweh raising as from the dead" (*God's Glory in Salvation through Judgment: A Biblical Theology* [Wheaton, IL: Crossway, 2010], 238).

17. The prophet Hosea is suspicious of the people's hearts even as they use language of repentance. He says their love is like a morning cloud or morning dew, which is temporary and quickly disappears (Hos. 6:4). Though Hosea isn't optimistic about the people's words in 6:1–2, their use of healing/resurrection imagery is the point for our purposes.

O Death, where are your plagues?

O Sheol, where is your sting?

Compassion is hidden from my eyes. (Hos. 13:14)

The promise in that verse is redemption from death. The power of Sheol will be rendered impotent. While the near-horizon fulfillment for the Israelites would be their corporate deliverance from the death of exile, the imagery assumes the power of God that conquers death through resurrection.

We know for sure that the far-horizon fulfillment of Hosea 13:14 was a future resurrection, for Paul cites this prophecy in a letter to the Corinthians while talking about resurrection. Paul writes, "When the perishable puts on the imperishable, and the mortal puts on immortality, then shall come to pass the saying that is written:

"Death is swallowed up in victory."

"O death, where is your victory?

O death, where is your sting?" (1 Cor. 15:54–55)

The "saying that is written" pulls together language from Isaiah 25:8 and Hosea 13:14. Death is personified in order to be mocked.

What can the power of Sheol do when faced with the power of God? This is the God who said, "'Let there be light,' and there was light" (Gen. 1:3). To the graves he will say, "Let there be life," and there will be life. God's work of redemption will not stop with the spirit, the inner man. The promise in Hosea 13:14 portrays resurrection as the redemption of bodies. The full application of what Jesus accomplished on the cross will mean our personal victory over death.

The Promise of Flourishing

Ever since the expulsion from Eden, mankind has faced the forces of death in the world through things like barrenness, famine, disease, destruction, and the grave. The work of God's lifegiving power on creation would bring reversal and renewal, even resurrection, and he alone can make this happen.

Through Hosea's prophecy, the Lord tells the Israelites,

> I will heal their apostasy;
> > I will love them freely,
> > for my anger has turned from them.
> I will be like the dew to Israel;
> > he shall blossom like the lily;
> > he shall take root like the trees of Lebanon;
> his shoots shall spread out;
> > his beauty shall be like the olive,
> > and his fragrance like Lebanon.
> They shall return and dwell beneath my shadow;
> > they shall flourish like the grain;
> they shall blossom like the vine;
> > their fame shall be like the wine of Lebanon.
> > (Hos. 14:4–7)

The God of life will be life to his people. And in the world full of death's effects, the power of life brings flourishing and vitality. Lilies blossom, roots grow, shoots spread, and beauty shines. The flourishing of creation is due to God's overriding blessing. And the thriving image-bearers are compared to a ruined creation being redeemed. If creation is to fully flourish, death must be overcome by the blessing of new life. God comes to make his blessings flow, far as the curse is found.

The Descent and Ascent of Jonah

In the literature of the Prophets, and among the Twelve, the last book we will consider is Jonah. The wayward prophet could not stay the hand of God. One way of talking about Jonah's story is with the language of descent. Jonah went down to Joppa (Jonah 1:3), down into a ship (1:3), then down into the ship's inner part (1:5). When the crew members determined that Jonah was the reason for the storm threatening their ship, they did what Jonah suggested and cast him overboard (1:12–15). Jonah descended into the sea, and then he descended into the belly of a great fish (1:17; 2:3, 6).

The prophet's ascent occurs when the fish vomited him onto dry land (2:10). Of his experience plummeting into the sea, Jonah recalls,

> the waters closed in over me to take my life;
> the deep surrounded me. (2:5)

His reflection depicts the approach of death:

> When my life was fainting away,
> I remembered the LORD,
> and my prayer came to you,
> into your holy temple. (2:7)

The fish rescued Jonah from drowning, but then he had to be rescued from the fish. The vomiting fish brought about Jonah's resurrection, figuratively speaking (see Heb. 11:20).[18]

The experience of Jonah in the fish lasted "three days and three nights" (Jonah 1:17), and the attentive Bible reader should see this as another example of a third-day deliverance. The descent and ascent of Jonah is a picture of death and resurrection, and this interpretation is confirmed by the words of Jesus himself: "For just as Jonah was three days and three nights in the belly of the great fish, so will the

---

18. As argued by Byron Wheaton, "This act of divine intervention when there was no human possibility of escaping death can only be understood as resurrection" ("As It Is Written: Old Testament Foundations for Jesus' Expectation of Resurrection," *Westminster Theological Journal* 70 [2008]: 252).

Son of Man be three days and three nights in the heart of the earth" (Matt. 12:40). Jesus speaks about his own coming deliverance from death by appealing to Jonah's deliverance.

Conclusion

The hope for resurrection grows stronger in the literature of the Prophets. God can end and return life. He can postpone death (as he did for Hezekiah) or prevent it altogether (as he did for Elijah). God's prophets were explicit about future resurrection as they spoke of him consuming death, redeeming bodies from death, and mocking the impotence of death. Stories of healing or rescue stoked the fire of hope that God would overcome all manifestations of the curse of sin. Multiple deliverances are marked by the third day. And prophetic oracles told of a time when God's creation would flourish by his lifegiving power.

3

Resurrection Hope in the Writings

If the Old Testament anticipates the death of death, then we should seek to see and understand all the ways that the biblical authors embed this hope. Indeed, some of the most dramatic pictures and prophecies of resurrection hope are found in the third and final section of the Old Testament, known as the Writings.

The literature of the Writings contains Psalms, Job, Proverbs, Ruth, Song of Solomon, Ecclesiastes, Lamentations, Esther, Daniel, Ezra-Nehemiah, and 1–2 Chronicles. The biblical authors advance resurrection hope through stories of rescue, explicit prophecies, wisdom sayings, songs of trust and thanksgiving, and return from exile.

Not Abandoned to Sheol

If the God of life will conquer death, then we should sing about that good news.[1] In the songs of Psalms, David has written about God's power and faithfulness to deliver his holy one.

---

1. Richard Bauckham says that a hope for resurrection life beyond death is found "especially in the Psalms" ("Life, Death, and the Afterlife in Second Temple Judaism," in *Life in the Face of Death: The Resurrection Message of the New Testament*, ed. Richard N. Longenecker [Grand Rapids, MI: Eerdmans, 1998], 85).

> Therefore my heart is glad, and my whole being rejoices;
>> my flesh also dwells secure.
> For you will not abandon my soul to Sheol,
>> or let your holy one see corruption.
> You make known to me the path of life;
>> in your presence there is fullness of joy;
>> at your right hand are pleasures forevermore.
>> (Ps. 16:9–11)

The holy one is not abandoned to death. God's man will walk the path of life and dwell secure in the fullness of joy and everlasting delight. Being delivered from the corruption of death means resurrection, so this resurrected state is crucial to experiencing the grandeur of what God has in store for his people. The Lord Jesus is the firstfruits of this glorified life.

When the apostle Peter preached to a Jerusalem crowd, he quoted Psalm 16 and applied the verses to Jesus, for Jesus is God's Holy One who did not see corruption. Jesus conquered death on the third day. Peter did not permit the words of this psalm to stop with its author David:

> Brothers, I may say to you with confidence about the patriarch David that he both died and was buried, and his tomb is with us to this day. Being therefore a prophet, and knowing that God had sworn with an oath to him that he would set one of his descendants on his throne, he foresaw and spoke about the resurrection of the Christ, that he was not abandoned to Hades, nor did his flesh see corruption. This Jesus God raised up, and of that we all are witnesses. (Acts 2:29–32)

Since Jesus rose to experience the fullness of glorified bodily life, we have that same hope in him. God will not abandon us. Our future resurrection is grounded in God's faithfulness and is made certain by our union with Christ. Because we were made to know God through embodied physicality, death will not thwart God's design.

Waking Up to Behold God's Face

In the prayer of David known as Psalm 17, the king calls on the Lord to "hear a just cause" and bring vindication (Ps. 17:1–2). David wants shelter from the wicked who oppose him and are ready to ambush and commit violence (17:8–12). He prays for deliverance by God's hand (17:13–14).[2] The wicked are those with a portion in this life only (17:14). "As for me," says David,

> I shall behold your face in righteousness;
>> when I awake, I shall be satisfied with your likeness.
>   (17:15)

Though the wicked can expect nothing good beyond this life, David looks with hope to what is in store for him: beholding the face of God. This glorious vision cannot occur in a fallen world through a fallen body, but God will make ready an existence that can behold glory. The beatific vision is a blessing of the resurrection. David's hope is to wake up after death and be satisfied with this glorious vision. This waking up is resurrection.[3] According to Geerhardus Vos, "The words

---

2. "Some of Israel's psalms indicate that death is something more than a biological event that occurs when the heart stops beating. . . . [I]n the view of Israel's psalmists, death's power is at work in us now, during our historical existence. Death's power is felt in the midst of life to the degree that one experiences any weakening of personal vitality through illness, bodily handicap, imprisonment, attack from enemies, or advancing old age. Any threat to a person's welfare . . . that is, one's freedom to be and to participate in the covenant community, is understood as an invasion of Death, regarded as a mythical Power, into 'the land of the living.' In some of the psalms (especially individual psalms of thanksgiving), one can see how the experience of salvation from the power of death moves toward the experience of 'resurrection,' that is, being restored from death to life" (Bernard W. Anderson, with Steven Bishop, *Contours of Old Testament Theology* [Minneapolis: Fortress, 1999], 312).

3. The Hebrew term for "awake" is used in other passages of resurrection (such as 2 Kings 4:31; Isa. 26:19; Dan. 12:2).

are unique within the limits of the Old Testament and so striking that we need not hesitate to find here also the thought of the resurrection."[4]

Ransomed from the Power of Sheol

Both the wise and the fool die (Ps. 49:10–12). The psalmist says,

> Like sheep they are appointed for Sheol;
>> death shall be their shepherd,
> and the upright shall rule over them in the morning.
>> Their form shall be consumed in Sheol, with no
>>> place to dwell.
> But God will ransom my soul from the power of Sheol,
>> for he will receive me. (49:14–15)

The righteous can hope they will be raised to life. The power of Sheol will be broken, and God will receive his people. This receiving is after death because the person is in Sheol's grip, but the power of God will ransom the soul by raising the body. The phrase "ransom . . . from the power of Sheol" is found elsewhere only in Hosea 13:14, so the prophet Hosea's words probably depend on the poet in Psalm 49:15. The verb translated "receive" (49:15) is the same one used to describe Enoch and Elijah being taken by the Lord (Gen. 5:24; 2 Kings 2:3). Though God received Enoch and Elijah before death, the singer in Psalm 49 has a resurrection hope that God will receive him after death.

Brought Up from the Depths

The psalmist remembers learning about the Lord from his youth, and at present he still proclaims God's wonders (Ps. 71:17). Because

---

4. Geerhardus Vos, *The Eschatology of the Old Testament*, ed. James T. Dennison, Jr. (Phillipsburg, NJ: P&R, 2001), 16.

he has already experienced the Lord's faithfulness, he prays for more of the same:

> So even to old age and gray hairs,
>> O God, do not forsake me,
> until I proclaim your might to another generation,
>> your power to all those to come. (71:18)

The psalmist wants to make known the truths of God to the next generation. He will experience, from youth to old age, the faithfulness of God. And then he will die.

But death is not the end.

> You who have made me see many troubles and calamities
>> will revive me again;
> from the depths of the earth
>> you will bring me up again. (Ps. 71:20)

The motion—reviving, bringing up—denotes resurrection. The depths of the earth represent the grave, and so from the grave the Lord will raise his people. The psalmist has experienced sufferings and troubles but also God's faithfulness through it all. And neither these sufferings nor death will overcome the faithfulness of the Lord. Rather, the faithfulness of the Lord will be shown by the psalmist overcoming death.

Received to Glory

In a psalm of Asaph, the writer tells of God's goodness to his people and the eventual ruin that will befall the wicked. Unlike the wicked who do not know the Lord, the psalmist says,

> I am continually with you;
>> you hold my right hand.
> You guide me with your counsel,
>> and afterward you will receive me to glory.
>> (Ps. 73:23–24)

Asaph has known God's guidance in this life. God holds his hand, directing him with divine wisdom. Death will not pull the psalmist from God's grip. He confesses that "afterward"—after death—"you will receive me to glory." God's hold is also a pull, from this earthly life to glory. Death will not subvert our communion with the Lord.

For the believer, "to live is Christ, and to die is gain" (Phil. 1:21). Like in Psalm 49:15, to "receive" can mean "take" (which reminds us of Enoch and Elijah whom God took; see Gen. 5:24; 2 Kings 2:3). According to Wright, the psalmist "discovers that he is grasped by a love that will not let him go, a power that even death, and the dissolution of the body, cannot thwart."[5] God holds our hand, and his grasp is stronger than death. God is with us and does not forsake us after our last breath. Our hope is resurrection glory. God will take us there, into it, united to Christ.

A Plea for Life

In one of his songs, Asaph prayed,

> Restore us, O God;
>> let your face shine, that we may be saved! (Ps. 80:3)

The Israelites had turned from the Lord. Rescued from Egypt, they entered the promised land by God's power and plan (80:8–11). But the God who had given them the land was dispossessing them from

---

5. N. T. Wright, *The Resurrection of the Son of God*, Christian Origins and the Question of God, vol. 3 (Minneapolis: Fortress Press, 2003), 106.

it (80:12–13). The nation was floundering in its sin. The people were facing the consequences of the covenant curses.

So Asaph prayed for God's favor and for his enemies to fall.

> Then we shall not turn back from you;
>> give us life, and we will call upon your name!
> Restore us, O LORD God of hosts!
>> Let your face shine, that we may be saved!
>> (80:18–19)

The judgment on the Israelites was a corporate death. But death by exile would be followed by a return, a corporate resurrection. Asaph calls on the God of life: "Give us life, and we will call upon your name!" God's shining face is lifegiving. The day will come when God's shining countenance will transform our lowly bodies. He will give them life, and we will call on him with thanksgiving, praise, and exultation.

The Confidence of Job

Not a psalmist, though still a sufferer, the man Job endured much. He lost his children to death, his wife told him to curse the Lord, his body was afflicted with sores, and his friends blamed his problems on unrepentant sin.[6]

Despite these serious and wearisome obstacles, Job was confident that the Lord would vindicate him, even if this vindication didn't occur until the last day:

> For I know that my Redeemer lives,
>> and at the last he will stand upon the earth.
> And after my skin has been thus destroyed,

---

6. As Levenson explains, "Bereavement of progeny is the functional equivalent of death" (*Resurrection and the Restoration of Israel: The Ultimate Victory of the God of Life* [New Haven, CT: Yale University Press, 2006], 115).

> yet in my flesh I shall see God,
>   whom I shall see for myself,
>   and my eyes shall behold, and not another.
>   My heart faints within me! (Job 19:25–27)

The righteous sufferer referred to his death with the expression "after my skin has been thus destroyed" (19:26). Yet his hope is that the destruction of flesh will be followed by renewed flesh in which he shall behold his God: "Yet in my flesh I shall see God" (19:26). As Fyall explains, Job "expects the experience which follows to take place after his skin has wasted away in death."[7] Job's hope will be fulfilled in a glorified body.

The Final Flourishing of Job

When the beginning and end of Job's story are compared (Job 1–2; 42), the reader discerns the onset of tragedy and the eventual earthly restoration of what was lost. The narrator says, "And the LORD restored the fortunes of Job, when he had prayed for his friends. And the LORD gave Job twice as much as he had before. . . . And the LORD blessed the latter days of Job more than his beginning" (42:10, 12). Job had more money, children, and livestock than before the events that begin the book.

These latter days of Job's life are an escalation of blessings that followed distress and heartache. These blessings conquered the forces of death. When Job finally died, he was "an old man, and full of days" (Job 42:17).[8] God's surpassing blessing on Job's life foreshadows the

---

7. Robert S. Fyall, *Now My Eyes Have Seen You: Images of Creation and Evil in the Book of Job*, New Studies in Biblical Theology 12 (Downers Grove, IL: InterVarsity Press, 2002), 51. Fyall says, "It is indeed true that Job expresses pessimism and hopelessness about the world beyond the grave (see e.g. 3:11–19; 7:9–10; 10:20–22), but these are dramatic not theological statements and express what Job is feeling at that moment. Similarly, when the writer of Ecclesiastes says, 'All go to the same place; all come from dust, and to dust all return' (3:20), he is reflecting the perspective of life 'under the sun' and not giving a definitive statement about the destiny of the departed" (50).

8. Where the Masoretic Text (MT) ends, the Septuagint (LXX) does not. The LXX adds a postscript to the book: "and it is written that he will be raised again with those whom the Lord

truth that our sufferings are producing a greater glory that outweighs them all (2 Cor. 4:17). This greater glory involves a bodily existence that God is preparing for us (2 Cor. 4:18–5:5).

Any loss while in this earthly tent—the body—cannot compare to the greater gain in store for the people of God. Resurrection is vindication. In glorified flesh we will behold the Lord and dwell with him, our advocate and Redeemer. We shall not die but live, full of everlasting days.

Laying Hold of the Tree of Life

While Psalms and Job help us think wisely about life, the future, and the faithfulness of God, the book of Proverbs is permeated with wisdom for life in God's world. The path of wisdom is the path of life. The phrase "tree of life" appears in two Old Testament books: Genesis and Proverbs. When Solomon talks about wisdom as a tree of life, we are meant to think about that lifegiving tree that held out hope for immortal physicality to those who would eat its fruit. Solomon says of wisdom,

> Her ways are ways of pleasantness,
> and all her paths are peace.
> She is a tree of life to those who lay hold of her;
> those who hold her fast are called blessed.
> (Prov. 3:17–18)

The potency of Eden's life is available, in part, through wisdom. The blessing of knowing God and fearing God marks the wise and ensures their future life. The wise are those who are, even now, tasting wisdom's fruit. According to Waltke, the tree of life represents

---

raises up." Whoever translated Job into Greek wanted to leave no doubt that the text affirmed bodily resurrection, even if a postscript had to be added to drive home the point.

"perpetual healing" that confirms eternal life.[9] The fruit from the tree of life belongs to the wise because the wise are those who know God. The wise will rise on the appointed day of resurrection, and the life they tasted at salvation will be theirs forever in glory.

No Death on the Path of Righteousness

Sometimes the sage introduces a tension that only resurrection can solve. In Proverbs 12:28, he says,

> In the path of righteousness is life,
>> and in its pathway there is no death.

Now the living know that physical death is what happens to image-bearers under the sun. Our days are numbered, and our earthly journey ends at the grave. Since Solomon would never be so ignorant as to say that the righteous will not physically die, he must mean a death beyond this death and a life beyond this life.

If there is no death on the path of righteousness, that must mean the God of life will overcome the effects of sin and the curse for his people. Waltke says that for the righteous, "Salvation from the grave is more than being spared an untimely death, for otherwise the path of life is swallowed up by death, an unthinkable thought in Proverbs."[10] Solomon can say "there is no death" for the righteous because God will overrule the grave.

The Restoration of Naomi and Her Family

Before Solomon wrote his proverbs and before David wrote his psalms, the Lord's providence brought deliverance and life to the

---

9. Bruce K. Waltke, *The Book of Proverbs: Chapters 1–15*, New International Commentary on the Old Testament (Grand Rapids, MI: Eerdmans, 2004), 105. He adds, "We should presume, then, that symbol here also represents the inseparable notions of healing and immortality" (259).

10. Waltke, *The Book of Proverbs*, 634.

family of their ancestor Ruth. The book of Ruth is about a journey from being emptied to being restored, from loss to gain, from famine to fullness. An Israelite named Naomi faced the threat of her family line coming to an end. Her husband had died; her children had died. The land without enough food (Ruth 1:1) is paired with a widow without hope for the future (1:2–5).[11]

But the greater the distress, the more incredible the deliverance. After God's providence connects Naomi's daughter-in-law Ruth to a man named Boaz, their relationship eventually leads to marriage (2:1; 4:13). And their marriage leads to offspring. The Lord gave Ruth a son, and some women told Naomi, "Blessed be the LORD, who has not left you this day without a redeemer, and may his name be renowned in Israel! He shall be to you a restorer of life and a nourisher of your old age, for your daughter-in-law who loves you, who is more to you than seven sons, has given birth to him" (4:14–15). These women identified Ruth's newborn son as a life-nourisher, a redeemer, a life-restorer.

Though the opening of Ruth's story is about death, the end is about life. The restoration of Naomi's family line—through the birth of Obed, Ruth's son with Boaz—is an act of resurrection.[12]

A Time for Judgment

There's no denying it: the book of Ecclesiastes contains some grim statements about life under the sun. All people, and all beasts, are heading toward the same place (from an earthly perspective): the grave. And our days on earth are marked by toil and pain, confusion

---

11. Stephen Dempster observes, "The obstacles to genealogy now are not barren women but dead males" (*Dominion and Dynasty: A Theology of the Hebrew Bible*, New Studies in Biblical Theology 15 [Downers Grove, IL: InterVarsity Press, 2003], 191).

12. As Byron Wheaton interprets the end of Ruth's story, "Out of death and hopelessness, life has sprung up" ("As It Is Written: Old Testament Foundations for Jesus' Expectation of Resurrection," *Westminster Theological Journal* 70 [2008]: 251).

and frailty. Nothing lasts. The wicked seem to prosper. Injustice remains unchecked in many places. How does the sage comfort himself in light of all these difficulties? "I said in my heart, God will judge the righteous and the wicked, for there is a time for every matter and for every work" (Eccles. 3:17).

The righteous and the wicked will face the God who is just. And since the wicked do not always face the consequences in this life for their deeds, the sage must be referring to a judgment beyond this life. A future perspective is also meant when he writes, "Though a sinner does evil a hundred times and prolongs his life, yet I know that it will be well with those who fear God, because they fear before him. But it will not be well with the wicked, neither will he prolong his days like a shadow, because he does not fear before God" (Eccles. 8:12–13).

The righteous may face suffering and even endure the exploits of the wicked, but they can say confidently with the sage, "It will be well." The wicked may think themselves invincible and unaccountable, but for them it will *not* be well. Death is not the end. There is a coming judgment beyond death, and it is reasonable to see this hope in the larger biblical context of a judgment and resurrection of the dead. Through the resurrection of bodies, God will vindicate his people and hold the wicked accountable. The saints will be raised unto glory. All will be well.

Favor in the King's Sight

When the evil Haman contrived a plot to kill the Jews throughout the Persian Empire, Queen Esther was the right person in the right position at the right time. Mordecai convinced her to go to the king and intervene on behalf of her people, the Jews. This move was risky. If someone disrupted the king's court without being invited first, the king could put that person to death (Est. 4:11). Yet after some days of fasting, Esther went to the king's court anyway, ready to perish (4:16).

Esther entered the court of the palace on the third day, while the king was on his throne (5:1). "And when the king saw Queen Esther standing in the court, she won favor in his sight, and he held out to Esther the golden scepter that was in his hand. Then Esther approached and touched the tip of the scepter" (5:2). On the third day Esther was delivered from death.[13] And through her deliverance and the actions that followed, she ensured the deliverance of her people from death.

The Deliverance of the Jews from Death

Queen Esther convinced the king of Haman's plot against the Jews, and the king permitted the Jews to defend themselves on what would have been the appointed day of their annihilation (Est. 7–8). Rather than being destroyed, the Jews overcame their enemies (Est. 9).

Since the forces of death advance in this world through the rise of enemies, the Jews under Esther experienced a national resurrection when they defended their lives. Dumbrell is right: "Reversal seems the most important structural theme in Esther."[14] Haman, who thought he would prosper, was put to death (7:10). Esther, who knew she was risking her life by approaching the king unsolicited, was spared (5:1–2). The plot against the Jews, which involved death looming over them wherever they lived, collapsed into the delivering hand of God.

Out of the Fiery Furnace

The book of Daniel contains harrowing moments when God's people were preserved through the death-dealing efforts of pagan authorities. In Daniel 3, three Jews named Shadrach, Meshach, and

---

13. This third-day deliverance is reminiscent of earlier third-day deliverances (see Gen. 22:4; 2 Kings 20:5; Hos. 6:2; Jonah 1:17).

14. William J. Dumbrell, *The Faith of Israel: A Theological Survey of the Old Testament*, 2nd ed. (Grand Rapids, MI: Baker Academic, 2002), 300.

Abednego stood up to the pressure of King Nebuchadnezzar, saying, "Be it known to you, O king, that we will not serve your gods or worship the golden image that you have set up" (Dan. 3:18). So the king ordered them cast into a fiery furnace (3:19–23).

But the king soon noticed them walking around unbound and unhurt (3:24–25). He ordered the three captives to emerge, and when they did, "the fire had not had any power over the bodies of those men. The hair of their heads was not singed, their cloaks were not harmed, and no smell of fire had come upon them" (3:27). The only explanation for this miracle was God's power. Their bodies should have perished, but the God of life overcame the power of death.

Out of the Den of Lions

In addition to the picture of resurrection in the fiery furnace, Daniel was delivered from death. He refused to pray according to the instructions of a royal edict (Dan. 6:6–13), and so he faced execution for his faithfulness to God. But God knows how to deliver his faithful people.

Daniel was cast into a den of lions, a stone was rolled over the entrance, and the king sealed it with his signet for the night (6:16–17). The next morning, the king rushed to the den and discovered that Daniel was alive. He asked, "O Daniel, servant of the living God, has your God, whom you serve continually, been able to deliver you from the lions?" (6:20). Daniel confirmed that God had shut the lions' mouths so that he remained unharmed (6:22). In fact, like the three Jews who survived the furnace, "no kind of harm was found on him, because he had trusted in his God" (6:23; see 3:25, 27).

The deliverance of Daniel from the den of lions is a picture of resurrection.[15] The den was supposed to become his tomb, yet from

---

15. André Lacocque says, "Here, as in chapter 3, we find the essence of the resurrection, that is, less a phenomenon of a life after death as the triumph of life over death, of hope over despair" (*The Book of Daniel*, trans. David Pellauer [Atlanta: John Knox, 1979], 108).

the tomb Daniel arose. This rescue foreshadows our own deliverance from death. We will be raised from death without the slightest trace of harm or corruption. Our God, the God of Abraham and Isaac and Jacob, the God of Shadrach and Meshach and Abednego, the living God of Daniel, will rescue us.

Awakening to Life or Shame

According to Daniel 12:2, the future resurrection is the awakening of bodies from the dust. This verse is the most important resurrection statement in the Old Testament because it is the clearest. It is the culmination of previous hints and expressions, and it pertains to both the righteous and unrighteous.[16] Daniel learns from the Lord, "Many of those who sleep in the dust of the earth shall awake, some to everlasting life, and some to shame and everlasting contempt. And those who are wise shall shine like the brightness of the sky above; and those who turn many to righteousness, like the stars forever and ever" (12:2–3).

The existence of the righteous will be an embodied glory, a life made possible by the power of God on the future day of resurrection. There is an allusion in Daniel 12:2 to Isaiah 26:19: "Your dead shall live; their bodies shall rise. You who dwell in the dust, awake and sing for joy!" Awakening from the dust is present in both passages, and ultimately the language of dust comes from Genesis 3:19 ("for you are dust / and to dust you shall return").

While the righteous can hope for a resurrection to life, the unrighteous should dread a resurrection to judgment, "to shame and everlasting contempt" (Dan. 12:2). The wicked will be held accountable through an embodied judgment. The tombs of all will be emptied, and all will stand before the Lord. The wise will enter

---

16. According to Wright, "Any second-Temple Jew who pondered the book would find in 12:2–3 not a new and outlandish idea, unanticipated and unforeseen, but the crown of all that had gone before" (*The Resurrection of the Son of God*, 115).

everlasting flourishing, an embodied glory prepared from the foundation of the world. But the fool will not flourish in the presence of God. The fool will not shine in the reflection of God's countenance. For the fool there will be only shame and contempt, an embodied death that doesn't end.

Going Up to Jerusalem from Captivity

If we recognize the ordering of the Hebrew Bible in Jesus's day, from Genesis to 2 Chronicles, then the last verse of the last book has something to contribute to our exploration of resurrection hope in the Law, Prophets, and Writings. The people of the southern kingdom (known as Judah) had been exiled to Babylon where they dwelled in captivity for approximately seventy years. We have seen how exile is a corporate death and how the prophets foretold a corporate resurrection. The Old Testament ends by sounding that note of hope.

Cyrus was king of Persia, and he conquered Babylon. Through him the Lord would fulfill prophecies of deliverance. A proclamation was sent throughout the Persian kingdom: "Thus says Cyrus king of Persia, 'The Lord, the God of heaven, has given me all the kingdoms of the earth, and he has charged me to build him a house at Jerusalem, which is in Judah. Whoever is among you of all his people, may the Lord his God be with him. Let him go up'" (2 Chron. 36:23).

The land of Babylon had been the place of Israel's descent. Now the ascent would begin. The Israelites could "go up" to the land of their forefathers. The Old Testament does not end with exile but with hope. Dempster explains, "The note of promise is a directive from Cyrus for them to return to the land and rebuild the temple. . . . The Tanakh ends on a note of hope, pointing to the future."[17] The return of the nation will mean life from death.

---

17. Dempster, *Dominion and Dynasty*, 48–49.

Not only is the last verse in the Hebrew Bible full of hope, but the very last *word* is hope-giving. The verb translated "let him go up" is about rising, ascending. Through the appointed deliverer Cyrus, the Lord was calling the captive Israelites to come forth from their Babylonian graves as he breathed life into their nation, like dry bones coming together in a valley.

Conclusion

The sages and singers of Israel join the chorus of patriarchs and prophets to anticipate the deliverance of God's people from death. Stories of rescue and prayers of faith continue to stoke the fires of resurrection hope. The earth will not possess the dead forever. There is a time to live and a time to die, but there is also a time to rise. The God of life will wake the dead. The righteous and the wicked will come forth to face the living God. The righteous will know his everlasting favor and will shine to show it, but the wicked will know only shame, an allotment of contempt that they must rise from death to fully receive. According to the Law, Prophets, and Writings, to dust you shall return, and from dust you shall arise.

4

Resurrection Hope in the Gospels

The four Gospels present to us the serpent crusher and curse bearer.[1] He was born in Bethlehem, raised in Nazareth, and baptized in the Jordan River. He taught and ministered throughout the land of Israel, died outside Jerusalem on a cross, and rose from the dead on the third day as the firstfruits of resurrection glory. "This death and the following resurrection victory serve as a shockwave that moves out from Jerusalem and slowly awakens the world to a new beginning."[2] We need to look at the truths he taught, the wonders he performed, and the victory he accomplished.

The One in Whom Is Life

The incarnation was when the Word became flesh, and with that the wisdom, love, mercy, and life of God became flesh as well. "In him was life, and the life was the light of men" (John 1:4). Because of who

---

1. See Andrew David Naselli, *The Serpent and the Serpent Slayer*, Short Studies in Biblical Theology (Wheaton, IL: Crossway, 2020).
2. Kelly M. Kapic, *Embodied Hope: A Theological Meditation on Pain and Suffering* (Downers Grove, IL: IVP Academic, 2017), 80.

he is, his words are the words of life (John 6:68), and his way is the way of life (Matt. 7:14).

The ministry of Jesus invaded this world like light piercing the darkness. As he traveled throughout the promised land, his light dawned on the needy and the outcast. The helpless and the destitute were objects of his blessing. He pronounced beatitudes for the meek, the mourning, and the merciful. For people with eyes to truly see, his deeds demonstrated who he was and is.

But his claims reveal his identity as well. "I am the bread of life; whoever comes to me shall not hunger, and whoever believes in me shall never thirst" (John 6:35). He gives life without being depleted. "I am the light of the world. Whoever follows me will not walk in darkness, but will have the light of life" (8:12). His way is life and light because he is life and light. "I am the resurrection and the life. Whoever believes in me, though he die, yet shall he live, and everyone who lives and believes in me shall never die. Do you believe this?" (11:25–26). Jesus came to be the giver of life. This life would be sin-defeating and death-conquering.

The age of the resurrection has dawned in him. Do you believe this?

Miracles of Restoration

All four Gospels tell stories of the wonder-working Savior. The prophecies in Isaiah 35 looked toward a time when great reversals would take place:

> Then the eyes of the blind shall be opened,
>   and the ears of the deaf unstopped;
> then shall the lame man leap like a deer,
>   and the tongue of the mute sing for joy.
>   (Isa. 35:5–6)

This cluster of reversals characterized the ministry of Jesus. The presence of lame or mute people was a reminder that this world was not as it should be. Blind and deaf people, who hoped for healing from Jesus, were a visible sign of brokenness in this present age. Restoration was needed, and Jesus was the one to bring it.

There were miracles in the Old Testament but not of the scope that was in Jesus's ministry. Elijah and Elisha, for instance, performed miracles. Moses and Aaron were used by God to work wonders. The patriarchs had experienced the power of God. But the ministry of Jesus was such an escalation of wonders that all previous eras paled in comparison. Elijah and Elisha were rushing streams, but Jesus was Niagara Falls.

The hands of Jesus brought life. He touched a leper, and immediately the leprosy was cleansed (Matt. 8:3). He took away the fever of Peter's mother-in-law (Matt. 8:14–15). He gave a paralytic the ability to walk again (Matt. 9:6–7). He stopped a discharge of blood that had plagued a woman for many years (Matt. 9:20–22). He fed the hungry by multiplying loaves and fish (Matt. 14:13–21). He healed a man's withered hand (Mark 3:1–5). He opened the ears of a deaf man and fixed his speech too (Mark 7:34–37). He gave the blind their sight (Mark 10:51–52).

All the afflictions of this world were present in one way or another during the ministry of Jesus, and his power subdued them. The miracles of Jesus were acts of conquest over the curse and its effects. Sometimes the volume of his healing ministry was so strong that the Gospel narrator simply provides a summary like this: "Now when the sun was setting, all those who had any who were sick with various diseases brought them to him, and he laid his hands on every one of them and healed them" (Luke 4:40).

Delivered from Demons

The principalities of this world could not resist the Son of God. His conquests included the exorcism of demonic powers. Demonic possession was dehumanizing because the host behaved and spoke in ways that degraded God's image-bearer. In one case, a father explained that the demonic spirit seized his son and caused him to convulse and foam at the mouth (Luke 9:39). The spirit would "often cast him into fire and into water, to destroy him" (Mark 9:22).

On another occasion, Jesus encountered a demoniac living among the tombs (Mark 5:2–3). This graveyard backdrop associates demonic possession with death. Day and night the possessed man would cry out and cut himself (5:5). The host had been overcome by the spirit and behaved in ways that were frightening and abnormal (5:3–4). The man had to live exiled from the city, which meant alienation from his family and friends and religious community. The exorcism of demonic powers brought restoration to the afflicted person. Exorcism was lifegiving. The man left his dwelling among the tombs and began proclaiming what Jesus had done (5:20).

Raising People from Death

While Elijah and Elisha were dependent on God's power to work through them to revive the dead (1 Kings 17:17–24; 2 Kings 4:18–37; 13:20–21), the hands of Jesus were the hands of God. And the Gospel narrators report his power to restore life on multiple occasions.

First, Jesus raised a widow's son during a funeral procession. He told the mother, "Do not weep," and then he said to the dead boy, "Young man, I say to you, arise" (Luke 7:13–14). The boy rose and began to speak (7:15). Jesus, the fountain of life, was overflowing and pushing back the forces of death.

Second, Jesus raised the daughter of Jairus. He came to Jairus's home and said, "Do not weep, for she is not dead but sleeping" (Luke 8:52).[3] The depiction of death as sleep has Old Testament background

---

3. N. T. Wright says, "This hardly indicates a language-system in which 'sleep' is a regular and obvious metaphor for death, but it may well indicate, at least in the minds of those who

(Isa. 26:19; Dan. 12:2). And for Jesus, raising the dead is as easy as waking someone from sleep. "Child, arise," he said, and "her spirit returned" (Luke 8:54–55).

Third, Jesus raised his friend Lazarus from the dead. The widow's son had still been on the funeral bier, and the daughter of Jairus had still been at home. But Lazarus had already been in the tomb for more than three days. Jesus cried out with a loud voice, "Lazarus, come out," and Lazarus did (John 11:43–44). Before this miracle, Martha had expressed the expectation of other Jews when she said, "I know that he will rise again in the resurrection on the last day" (11:24). Jesus said, "I am the resurrection and the life" (11:25), and he proved it when he revived the dead. Martha's words were about that future resurrection, yet Jesus demonstrated that he could raise the dead before that last day when all the tombs would open.[4]

When All in the Tombs Will Hear Him

The deliverance of people from death during the ministry of Jesus was a foreshadowing of that final day when all the dead will be raised. Just as the widow's son and Jairus's daughter and Lazarus obeyed the voice of Jesus and revived, so also the tombs will open at the voice of Jesus. Disease and demons must submit to him, and his dominion will subdue death as well. Jesus said,

> Truly, truly, I say to you, an hour is coming, and is now here, when the dead will hear the voice of the Son of God, and those who hear will live. For as the Father has life in himself,

---

told or heard the story, a hint of Daniel 12.2, where those who 'sleep' will be woken up" (*The Resurrection of the Son of God*, Christian Origins and the Question of God, vol. 3 [Minneapolis: Fortress, 2003], 404).

4. Thomas Schreiner says, "The resurrection, as Martha clearly understands, is an eschatological event (11:24). Martha's understanding accords with the OT, for Daniel locates the resurrection (12:2) at 'the time of the end' (12:9)" (*The King in His Beauty: A Biblical Theology of the Old and New Testaments* [Grand Rapids, MI: Baker Academic, 2013], 518).

so he has granted the Son also to have life in himself. And he has given him authority to execute judgment, because he is the Son of Man. Do not marvel at this, for an hour is coming when all who are in the tombs will hear his voice and come out, those who have done good to the resurrection of life, and those who have done evil to the resurrection of judgment. (John 5:25–29)

These five verses may be the most significant statements Jesus ever made about the general resurrection. At the beginning of these verses, Jesus is teaching that there is true life here and now for sinners—the spiritual life which he alone gives.[5] He is bread and light, salvation and resurrection. In union with him, sinners live now, though outwardly they are still wasting away.

The end of these verses is about the coming bodily resurrection of all people. His words include believers and unbelievers because he speaks of "those who have done good" and "those who have done evil." That duality is the division of mankind based on what people have done with Jesus. If Jesus is their Savior, they will be raised "to the resurrection of life." If Jesus is not their Savior, then he is their Judge, and they will be raised "to the resurrection of judgment."

The language in John 5:29 alludes to Daniel 12:2, for that Old Testament verse is the clearest expression of the future resurrection—for both the righteous and the wicked—that will establish everlasting states. The power that God's Son has displayed in the promised land is certainly impressive and mindboggling, but it will be surpassed in scope when he gives life to all the dead that have ever lived. Do you believe this?

---

5. G. K. Beale writes, "John 5:24–29 sees the resurrection of the saints predicted in Dan. 12:2 as being inaugurated in Jesus' ministry" (*The Book of Revelation*, New International Greek Testament Commentary [Grand Rapids, MI: Eerdmans, 1998], 434).

Rising Up at the Judgment

Jesus taught that the future judgment occurs after the resurrection of the dead. The dead will be gathered for judgment. Jesus rebuked his contemporary generation for such widespread rejection and skepticism of his ministry and identity. And he warned them that they would face judgment:

> The men of Nineveh will rise up at the judgment with this generation and condemn it, for they repented at the preaching of Jonah, and behold, something greater than Jonah is here. The queen of the South will rise up at the judgment with this generation and condemn it, for she came from the ends of the earth to hear the wisdom of Solomon, and behold, something greater than Solomon is here. (Matt. 12:41–42)

Looking carefully at the language, we notice that the "men of Nineveh" and the "queen of the South" represent those who know the Lord, and "this generation" represents those who do not know the Lord. These groups, however, will "rise up" together at the judgment. Jesus, who is greater than Jonah and greater than Solomon, will hold the nations to account. This promise of rising and judgment is parallel in meaning to John 5:28–29 and reflects the influence of Daniel 12:2. Jesus warns that the wicked will rise for judgment because he believes what the Old Testament teaches.

Gathering All the Nations

The coming judgment and resurrection are associated with glory and authority:

> When the Son of Man comes in his glory, and all the angels with him, then he will sit on his glorious throne. Before him

will be gathered all the nations, and he will separate people one from another as a shepherd separates the sheep from the goats. And he will place the sheep on his right, but the goats on the left. (Matt. 25:31–33)

Jesus will gather the nations by resurrection. Raising the nations will lead to judging the nations. The placements of people on the "right" and "left" signify their differing eternal states. The righteous will be raised for everlasting life, and the wicked will be raised for everlasting punishment (25:46).[6] The wicked will depart from the Lord into "the eternal fire prepared for the devil and his angels" (25:41). The saints will "inherit the kingdom prepared for [them] from the foundation of the world" (25:34).

One purpose of resurrection for God's people, therefore, is that they might inherit, as embodied image bearers, all that God has prepared for them. God's children will not remain disembodied heirs. The glory before us is too great; the kingdom too glorious. Such coming glory can only be received by people who are themselves glorified.

Shining Like the Sun in the Kingdom

The future glorious state of God's people is depicted in a parable. In Jesus's parable of the weeds, he taught that seeds and weeds grow together in the field of this world until the time of reaping, known as the harvest at the end of the age. On that day, the weeds will be separated from the harvest and cast into the fire (Matt. 13:40–42). This casting represents the eternal judgment of the wicked.

---

6. According to Murray Harris, "Of course the details of the picture cannot be pressed, but the phrases . . . more easily comport with the idea of judgment on resurrected persons than with judgment on disembodied spirits" (*Raised Immortal: Resurrection and Immortality in the New Testament* [Grand Rapids, MI: Eerdmans, 1985], 174–75).

Jesus said, "Then the righteous will shine like the sun in the kingdom of their Father" (Matt. 13:43). He thus described the righteous in language alluding to Daniel 12:3: "And those who are wise shall shine like the brightness of the sky above; and those who turn many to righteousness, like the stars forever and ever."[7] For the righteous, rising leads to shining because of the power of God endowing his embodied image-bearers with glory and honor.

A Whole Body Going Into Hell

In Jesus's Sermon on the Mount, he warned about the future of those who don't take the battle against sin seriously. He said,

> If your right eye causes you to sin, tear it out and throw it away. For it is better that you lose one of your members than that your whole body be thrown into hell. And if your right hand causes you to sin, cut it off and throw it away. For it is better that you lose one of your members than that your whole body go into hell. (Matt. 5:29–30)

Jesus's words about the body being thrown into hell imply the resurrection of the dead, specifically the raising of the wicked.[8] Though unbelievers die physically, their bodies have a future. In order for the whole body to be cast into hell, that dead body must be raised. And the raising, in this case, is for judgment because the location of the whole body will be hell. This judgment fulfills Daniel 12:2, where the prophet hears that God will raise "some to shame and everlasting contempt."

When Jesus said, "And do not fear those who kill the body but cannot kill the soul. Rather fear him who can destroy both soul and

---

7. Schreiner, *The King in His Beauty*, 444.
8. According to Harris, "The possibility that the 'whole body' may be thrown into Gehenna . . . certainly suggests a resurrection to condemnation" (*Raised Immortal*, 174).

body in hell" (Matt. 10:28), his teaching parallels Matthew 5:29–30. He warned about the bodily judgment of the wicked.[9] Their everlasting state is not disembodied, even though the bodies of the wicked die now in this present age. As Craig Keener explains, "Mortals can destroy only one's body, but God can resurrect the body for damnation and destroy the whole person."[10]

Repaid at the Resurrection

While dining with a ruler of the Pharisees, Jesus emphasized the inclusion of outcasts so that the host could show hospitality without being repaid. Jesus said,

> When you give a dinner or a banquet, do not invite your friends or your brothers or your relatives or rich neighbors, lest they also invite you in return and you be repaid. But when you give a feast, invite the poor, the crippled, the lame, the blind, and you will be blessed, because they cannot repay you. For you will be repaid at the resurrection of the just. (Luke 14:12–14)

The blessing on such a host would be received through the future resurrection. If the host had a hospitable heart for the outcast and downtrodden, he would be demonstrating a love of neighbor that accords with "the just." And the just will be raised unto life and blessing.

Jesus's reference to the "resurrection of the just" holds out future hope as a motivator for present generosity and hospitality toward those who cannot offer repayment. The host would be repaid at the

---

9. According to Grant Osborne, in Matt. 10:28, "Jesus followed Daniel 12:2 regarding the resurrection of good and evil alike" ("Resurrection," in *Dictionary of Jesus and the Gospels* [Downers Grove, IL: InterVarsity Press, 1992], 676).

10. Craig S. Keener, *A Commentary on the Gospel of Matthew* (Grand Rapids, MI: Eerdmans, 1999), 326.

resurrection of the just, which would be a blessing surpassing any kind of repayment offered here on earth.

No Marriage in the Resurrection

During the week of Jesus's passion and death, he taught in the temple courts about the nature of resurrection life in the age to come. His teaching was in response to a gotcha question from the Sadducees. They denied a hope of bodily resurrection, and they wanted to portray it as absurdly as possible. They described the following scenario: through levirate marriage (see Deut. 25:5–10), a woman married the seven brothers in a family with the goal of raising up offspring, yet each husband died without any children being born. The Sadducees said, "In the resurrection, therefore, of the seven, whose wife will she be? For they all had her" (Matt. 22:28).

According to Jesus, the mistake of the Sadducees here was twofold: "You are wrong, because you know neither the Scriptures nor the power of God" (22:29). They didn't believe that the Torah (which was the Scripture they recognized as authoritative) held out any hope for a resurrection from the dead—but they were wrong. They also assumed that life in the age to come would be just like life in the present age. If there is marriage now, there must be marriage later.

But the nature of resurrection life has a discontinuity that the Sadducees did not discern. "For in the resurrection they neither marry nor are given in marriage, but are like angels in heaven" (22:30). The saints will be like the heavenly angels in the sense that they will be unmarried. Since marriage is an earthly covenant for this life only, the hypothetical scenario from the Sadducees was meaningless. The widow who married all seven brothers successively would be raised to a life where there is no marriage.

The God of the Living

The Sadducees should have learned from the Torah that God is "not God of the dead, but of the living" (Matt. 22:32). The patriarchs—Abraham, Isaac, and Jacob—had been gathered to their people at death, but death was not the end of their life. The covenant God whom they served would raise them. His blessings would overcome all aspects of fallenness and the curse—including death. Would the God of the covenant reverse the corruption of this world and leave death undone?

Jesus pointed the Sadducees to the book of Exodus. "And as for the resurrection of the dead, have you not read what was said to you by God: 'I am the God of Abraham, and the God of Isaac, and the God of Jacob'?" (Matt. 22:31–32, citing Ex. 3:6). Resurrection hope is reasonable in light of the covenant God who is life and gives life.[11] After all, God had enabled Abraham, Isaac, and Jacob to have offspring through wives who had been barren. These patriarchs had experienced the power of God in their families as he resurrected their family lines and advanced their progeny.

If the Sadducees had the spiritual discernment to read the Torah with understanding, they would have seen the God of life continually at work against the forces of death.

Prophesying a Third-Day Resurrection

The disciples of Jesus heard him teach on at least a few occasions that he was going to be rejected, suffer at the hands of others, be killed, and rise from the dead. In Matthew 17, he put it this way: "The Son

---

11. According to Brandon Crowe, "Though Exodus 3 does not include the terminology of resurrection, Jesus's argument assumes that God's covenantal promises to the patriarchs remain in force, even though the patriarchs died (cf. Luke 20:28). If the latter is true, then it must mean that God will fulfill his promises to the patriarchs; this time of fulfillment must refer to the resurrection age" (*The Hope of Israel: The Resurrection of Christ in the Acts of the Apostles* [Grand Rapids, MI: Baker Academic, 2020], 155).

of Man is about to be delivered into the hands of men, and they will kill him, and he will be raised on the third day" (Matt. 17:22–23).

In the four Gospels, Jesus not only taught a future resurrection of the dead for all people at his return, he taught that he himself would be raised from the dead in the middle of human history. He would be the pioneer of resurrection life and glory. He would be the first to shine in the way Daniel 12:2–3 describes. He would inaugurate the new creation work of God in his victory over death.

Notice that he specified the "third day." Given the multiple instances of third-day deliverances in the Old Testament (like Isaac, Hezekiah, Jonah, or Esther), Jesus's prophecy connects to that pattern and will fulfill it. Though his disciples, like other faithful readers of the Old Testament, would have expected a general resurrection of the dead at an appointed time, they were not expecting one man to inaugurate the resurrection by his own vindication in history.

Tombs Opening at the Death of Jesus

The crucifixion of Jesus was associated with miraculous events. From noon to three, "there was darkness over all the land" (Matt. 27:45), and "the curtain of the temple was torn in two, from top to bottom" when Jesus died (27:51). Matthew's Gospel is unique with what else it reports: "The tombs also were opened. And many bodies of the saints who had fallen asleep were raised, and coming out of the tombs after his resurrection they went into the holy city and appeared to many" (27:52–53).

The death of Jesus caused resurrection—the resurrection of bodies in tombs.[12] The number of the saints who were raised is not given,

---

12. According to Matthew Thiessen, "What is most shocking about this portrayal is that at the very moment that the forces of impurity seem to have finally beaten Jesus, at the precise instant that Jesus becomes a corpse and presumably a source of corpse contamination, holy power emanates out of him and into the abode of death—tombs—to snatch away bodies who were themselves sources of ritual impurity. Whereas corpses usually emit some miasma of impurity,

nor are their names, nor are we told how long they lived until they died again. But Matthew does say that these saints remained alive in their tombs until after Jesus's resurrection, and at that point they entered Jerusalem and appeared to many.

Several Old Testament passages may serve as background for this account. First, in 2 Kings 13:21, Elisha was already dead when contact with his bones caused the resurrection of a man. In an escalated way, the death of Jesus brought about the resurrection of many bodies that had died. Second, in Isaiah 26:19, we are told,

> Your dead shall live; their bodies shall rise.
> You who dwell in the dust, awake and sing for joy!
> For your dew is a dew of light,
> and the earth will give birth to the dead.

At the death of Jesus, the tombs of the earth birthed many people back to life. They had "fallen asleep" (Matt. 27:52), and now they awoke (Isa. 26:19). Third, in Ezekiel 37:12, God tells the prophet, "Therefore prophesy, and say to them, Thus says the Lord God: Behold, I will open your graves and raise you from your graves, O my people. And I will bring you into the land of Israel." In Matthew 27:52–53, the graves were opened, and the inhabitants entered Jerusalem. Fourth, in Daniel 12:2, the heavenly messenger says, "And many of those who sleep in the dust of the earth shall awake, some to everlasting life, and some to shame and everlasting contempt." Matthew reports that "many" who had "fallen asleep" rose from the dead.[13]

Jesus's corpse appears to emit a miasma of holy power that selectively revivifies long-dead saints. This holy discharge is wide-ranging, traveling from Jesus's corpse at Golgotha to and through Jerusalem. It is also unspeakably powerful, reaching deep into the bowels of death to give life to those who have been long dead. Matthew narrates in dramatic fashion how Jesus's crucifixion is ultimately a victory over death itself" (*Jesus and the Forces of Death: The Gospels' Portrayal of Ritual Impurity Within First-Century Judaism* [Grand Rapids, MI: Baker Academic, 2020], 111).

13. Wright, *The Resurrection of the Son of God*, 633.

These four passages—2 Kings 13, Isaiah 26, Ezekiel 37, and Daniel 12—inform the account in Matthew 27:52–53. Interpreters should not conclude that this mysterious and unique event fulfills the Old Testament passages, but it does connect to them in a way that strengthens the hope in the passages. The event also confirms the significance of Jesus's death. Though many people had been crucified before and would be after Jesus, what happened on that cross carried a power and a glory that was not obvious at the time. The cross displayed strength in weakness and glory in humiliation. The onlookers did not realize they were watching the death of death in the death of Christ.

The Empty Tomb of Jesus

The third day brought the dawn of something new. The glorious life of the age to come had invaded a tomb. The body inside—once riddled with suffering, agony, and finally death—awoke. The breath of life filled his lungs and then filled the room.

By the time the women arrived to anoint Jesus's body, he was gone. The stone had been rolled back, and an angel told them, "Do not be afraid, for I know that you seek Jesus who was crucified. He is not here, for he has risen, as he said. Come, see the place where he lay" (Matt. 28:5–6). When the women told the disciples what had happened and what the angel had said, Peter and John raced to the tomb (John 20:4). They, too, found it empty. Then they returned home.

As Mary stood outside the tomb, a voice asked her, "Woman, why are you weeping? Whom are you seeking?" (John 20:15). She thought the voice was the gardener's. She did not realize Jesus had spoken to her. And yet Jesus was, in a more important sense, a gardener indeed (see Gen. 2:15). He was the last Adam, not returning to dust but risen and tending to matters of new creation. He said, "Mary," and then she realized who was with her (John 20:16). Later she announced to the disciples, "I have seen the Lord" (20:18). A bodily resurrection had occurred.[14] The body of Jesus was missing from the tomb because he had risen, just as he had said. Because he lives, we shall also live. Something greater than death is here.

On the Road to Emmaus

The risen Jesus drew near to two men who were walking to a village called Emmaus (Luke 24:13–15). "But their eyes were kept from recognizing him" (24:16). Though the men did not discern his identity, we should not conclude that he did not look like Jesus. Their eyes "were kept" from recognizing him, and the purpose for this was the revelatory events that followed.

The two men recounted what had happened:

> Moreover, some women of our company amazed us. They were at the tomb early in the morning, and when they did not find his body, they came back saying that they had even seen a vision of angels, who said that he was alive. Some of those who were with us went to the tomb and found it just as the women had said, but him they did not see. (24:22–24).

News about the empty tomb was spreading. In the home of the men, Jesus ate with them and "took the bread and blessed and broke it and gave it to them. And their eyes were opened, and they recognized him. And he vanished from their sight" (24:30–31). The men had observed their companion walking with them, talking with

---

14. According to L. Michael Morales, "As with the historical exodus of Israel out of Egypt, the new exodus is the deliverance of God's firstborn Son from death. . . . As all living things emerged out of the ark with Noah, so an entire new creation emerges out of the tomb in the resurrection of Jesus Christ" (*Exodus Old and New: A Biblical Theology of Redemption* [Downers Grove, IL: IVP Academic, 2020], 172, 188).

them, and sitting to eat with them. But there was something unusual about his body, because when they recognized his identity, he disappeared. The risen body of Jesus was capable of acts that did not characterize mortal flesh.

The Flesh and Bones of Jesus

As the men from the road to Emmaus shared with the disciples in Jerusalem about the things that had happened, Jesus himself appeared and stood among them. "But they were startled and frightened and thought they saw a spirit" (Luke 24:37). Such a sudden appearance was not normal behavior for a body. A person needed to use a door or another opening!

Jesus said, "See my hands and my feet, that it is I myself. Touch me, and see. For a spirit does not have flesh and bones as you see that I have" (24:39). His words drew attention to the fact that an actual body was among his disciples. They were not seeing a disembodied phantom. They were seeing the risen Jesus in an imperishable body, and this body was able to do what their own bodies could not.

Yet the risen body of Jesus had continuity with what they knew of him before his death. He said, "Have you anything here to eat?" (24:41). They gave Jesus some fish, which he took and ate in front of them (24:42–43). This further confirmed the bodily nature of his presence.

Jesus took that opportunity to teach them. He opened their minds to understand the Old Testament and said, "Thus it is written, that the Christ should suffer and on the third day rise from the dead" (24:46). The disciples were witnesses of Scripture being fulfilled. The Christ who had suffered was now risen before their very eyes.

Breakfast by the Sea

On another occasion Jesus revealed himself again to his disciples. As day was dawning across the Sea of Galilee, "Jesus stood on the shore; yet the disciples did not know that it was Jesus" (John 21:4). This observation suggests that Jesus in his risen body could sometimes be discerned and other times not. But once he directed those in the boat to cast their nets on the right side so that they caught a great quantity of fish, the disciples realized who stood on the shore (John 21:6–8).

When they came to shore, Jesus invited them to have breakfast with him (John 21:12). He gave them bread and fish, and they ate together. This revelation, like the preceding ones, showed the truth of Jesus's humanity. The risen Jesus could stand with them, talk with them, and eat with them. This meal with Christ foreshadowed the day when all the nations shall feast together in the presence of the Lord of hosts (Isa. 25:6). He will take away their reproach and wipe away their tears (Isa. 25:8). Do you believe this?

Conclusion

The narratives in the four Gospels introduce us to the one who would bear our sins on the cross and rise from the dead on the third day. His teachings affirmed a future resurrection for the righteous and the wicked, but he himself was raised in the middle of history as the firstfruits of the life that will be ours. At his return he will call to the tombs, and all will come forth. The wicked will experience an unending embodied judgment, but we, as the saints of God, will enter the joy and glory that is ours in Christ. Union with Christ means that because he lives, we will live. The lifegiving power of the Son of God will transform our perishable and vulnerable state. We will shine like the sun—and like the Son.

5

Resurrection Hope in Acts

The apostles taught and ministered in the name of the risen Jesus. After the ascension of the Lord, the word of God spread from Jerusalem as the apostles obeyed Jesus and experienced persecution. Their words and deeds were reminiscent of Jesus himself, teaching a resurrection hope and reviving dead people to life. Integral to the preaching of these apostles was the Lord's third-day resurrection.

The Bodily Ascension of Jesus

According to the Old Testament books of Genesis and 2 Kings, both Enoch and Elijah ascended to the Lord without first dying. With the ascension of Jesus, we are reminded of Enoch and Elijah, yet Jesus ascended after he had died and risen. Forty days after rising from death, "he was lifted up, and a cloud took him out of their sight" (Acts 1:9).

The taking up of Christ was more important than what happened with Enoch and Elijah, because his humanity was now imperishable, immortal. The resurrection of Jesus reunited his spirit and body, and he was raised never to die again. His glorified state was not merely for earth. His resurrection was for the preparation of humanity to inherit the kingdom.

Jesus rose bodily, ascended bodily, reigns bodily, and will return bodily. "And while they were gazing into heaven as he went, behold, two men stood by them in white robes, and said, 'Men of Galilee, why do you stand looking into heaven? This Jesus, who was taken up from you into heaven, will come in the same way as you saw him go into heaven'" (Acts 1:10–11). The Jesus who rose in a glorified body will forever dwell as the Word made flesh.[1]

Christ's ascension to heaven now comprises part of the believer's hope because "our citizenship is in heaven, and from it we await a Savior, the Lord Jesus Christ, who will transform our lowly body to be like his glorious body, by the power that enables him even to subject all things to himself" (Phil. 3:20–21).

Impossible for Death to Hold Him

After Christ's ascent, the Spirit came on the disciples and others who had gathered in a home on the day of Pentecost (Acts 2:1–4). The Spirit empowered the disciples and enabled their message to be understood by those who spoke different languages.

Peter's sermon on Pentecost in Jerusalem has various points that connect to our study of resurrection hope. First, he made summary statements about the ministry of Jesus:

> Men of Israel, hear these words: Jesus of Nazareth, a man attested to you by God with mighty works and wonders and signs that God did through him in your midst, as you yourselves know—this Jesus, delivered up according to the definite plan and foreknowledge of God, you crucified and killed

---

1. For an excellent study of the ascension, see Patrick Schreiner, *The Ascension of Christ: Recovering a Neglected Doctrine* (Bellingham, WA: Lexham, 2020).

by the hands of lawless men. God raised him up, loosing the pangs of death, because it was not possible for him to be held by it. (Acts 2:22–24)

Jesus did the works of God according to the plan of God, and God vindicated him by resurrection. Peter announced the impossibility that death could hold Jesus.

Second, Peter explained how Jesus's resurrection fulfilled Scripture. In Psalm 16, David had written with hope about not being abandoned to Sheol, about the Holy One of God not seeing corruption (Ps. 16:8–11). Yet David died, so David's words were not primarily about him; they were about another. Peter said,

Brothers, I may say to you with confidence about the patriarch David that he both died and was buried, and his tomb is with us to this day. Being therefore a prophet, and knowing that God had sworn with an oath to him that he would set one of his descendants on his throne, he foresaw and spoke about the resurrection of the Christ, that he was not abandoned to Hades, nor did his flesh see corruption. (Acts 2:29–31)

Jesus is the new David who was delivered from bodily corruption. The tomb of David was occupied, but the tomb of Jesus was empty.

Third, Peter linked the events of Jesus's resurrection and ascension:

This Jesus God raised up, and of that we all are witnesses. Being therefore exalted at the right hand of God, and having received from the Father the promise of the Holy Spirit, he has poured out this that you yourselves are seeing and hearing. For David did not ascend into the heavens, but he himself says,

> "'The Lord said to my Lord,
> "Sit at my right hand,
>   until I make your enemies your footstool.'"
>   (Acts 2:32–35)

The reign of the risen Christ is through his ascension to the Father.

The news of Christ's resurrection and reign is good news for us, because our union with Christ means deliverance from corruption as well. And when we rise, we will reign with him. At the right hand of God, Jesus dwells in immortal, bodily life as he subdues his enemies, and that includes the last enemy, which is death.

The Author of Life Whom God Raised

After the healing of a lame man in front of a gate to the temple (Acts 3:1–10), Peter addressed a gathering of people and insisted that it was not by his or John's power or piety that the lame man was healed. The healing was accomplished in the name of the risen Jesus. Peter said,

> The God of Abraham, the God of Isaac, and the God of Jacob, the God of our fathers, glorified his servant Jesus, whom you delivered over and denied in the presence of Pilate, when he had decided to release him. But you denied the Holy and Righteous One, and asked for a murderer to be granted to you, and you killed the Author of life, whom God raised from the dead. To this we are witnesses. (3:13–15)

The rejection and murder of Jesus was the rejection and murder of the very "Author of life." Peter proclaimed Jesus's resurrection. That third-day deliverance was when God "glorified his servant Jesus" (3:13). It was by the power of the glorified Jesus—and in his name—that Peter had addressed the lame man. And the lifegiving power of the risen Jesus enabled the lame man to walk (3:6–8).

Raising Up a Prophet Like Moses

While Peter was still speaking in the context of the lame man's healing, he mentioned a hope from the Torah and applied it to the good news about Jesus.

> Moses said, "The Lord God will raise up for you a prophet like me from your brothers. You shall listen to him in whatever he tells you. And it shall be that every soul who does not listen to that prophet shall be destroyed from the people." And all the prophets who have spoken, from Samuel and those who came after him, also proclaimed these days. (Acts 3:22–24)

Peter was talking about "these days" as the days when the longed-for prophet had been sent and raised up. Peter drew from Deuteronomy 18:15–19. God's promise was to bring a prophet to the people, and this prophet would speak the very words of God. Rejecting this prophet's words meant judgment.

As Peter interpreted Deuteronomy 18, he rightly saw that God would raise up the appointed prophet *from the dead*. Peter told his audience,

> You are the sons of the prophets and of the covenant that God made with your fathers, saying to Abraham, "And in your offspring shall all the families of the earth be blessed."

God, having raised up his servant, sent him to you first, to bless you by turning every one of you from your wickedness. (Acts 3:25–26)[2]

Jesus is the agent of blessing for the families of the earth. He is the seed of Abraham. He is also the prophet whom God promised to raise up and whose mouth would speak words of life. Jesus is the prophet like Moses, and God raised him not just onto the stage of human history but from the grave.

The Risen Cornerstone

The religious leaders were "greatly annoyed" at the apostles because "they were teaching the people and proclaiming in Jesus the resurrection from the dead" (Acts 4:2). So Peter and John were held in custody, and on the next day they testified before the council of leaders. Peter told them,

Let it be known to all of you and to all the people of Israel that by the name of Jesus Christ of Nazareth, whom you crucified, whom God raised from the dead—by him this man is standing before you well. This Jesus is the stone that was rejected by you, the builders, which has become the cornerstone. (4:10–11)

---

2. Brandon Crowe argues, "The language of raising is particularly likely in this context of Acts 3 to evoke the raising of Jesus from the dead for at least four reasons. First, this statement is found in a context in which Peter expounds the resurrection of Jesus (cf. 3:13–21). Second, in 3:26 Peter explains that God has raised up (*anastesas*) Jesus (from the dead), which explains the way in which the raising up of a prophet like Moses in Deuteronomy 18 is fulfilled. Third, Deuteronomy 18:15 is also echoed in Luke 9:35 to underscore the eschatological message and mission of Jesus on the mount of transfiguration. The transfiguration of Jesus is organically tied to—indeed it is a preview of—Jesus's exalted, resurrected state. Jesus is the glorious, authoritative one to whom the people (including Moses and Elijah) must listen. Luke thus provides several indications that the application of Deuteronomy 18 to Jesus entails Jesus being raised up—from the dead—as the bearer of eschatological life and glory. Fourth, as with earlier speeches, the emphasis on Jesus's resurrection is designed to elicit a response. In this case, Peter explains that the raising up of Jesus is designed for blessing, that the covenant people might repent (3:26)" (*The Hope of Israel: The Resurrection of Christ in the Acts of the Apostles* [Grand Rapids, MI: Baker Academic, 2020], 37–38).

Peter's message to the religious leaders was the same as his message to the crowds in the city. The religious leaders had opposed Jesus, and in a sense of corporate identity, the people of Israel had rejected the one who had come to save them. Yet by the rejection of the messianic stone, God established Jesus as the cornerstone through his resurrection from the dead.[3] Now God offered "repentance to Israel and forgiveness of sins" (5:31). This reconciliation was possible because the Jesus whom God raised was exalted "at his right hand as Leader and Savior" (5:31).

Dorcas Restored to Life

In the book of Acts, we can see how the miracles of Jesus are echoed in the miracles of the apostles. The healing of the lame man in Acts 3 is an example of this, as is the restoration of Dorcas in Acts 9. Dorcas became ill and died, and she was laid in an upper room (Acts 9:37). Peter arrived, knelt beside her, and addressed her with her Aramaic name, "Tabitha, arise." She opened her eyes, life restored (9:39–40).

The resurrection of Dorcas reminds us of Lazarus, the widow's son, and Jairus's daughter. And her resurrection reminds us of the people who were restored during the ministries of Elijah and Elisha. Like all these who had received life again, Dorcas was restored to her mortal body. It was Jesus's body that rose glorified, and only at his return will his people be raised to an imperishable state.

Appointed as Judge of the Living and the Dead

After the resurrection of Dorcas, the Lord arranged the meeting of Peter and a man named Cornelius, who was a God-fearing Gentile. Peter said to Cornelius,

---

3. Crowe explains, "This is another example of a psalm being used messianically, again in relation to the resurrection. The rejected stone corresponds to the crucifixion of the Messiah, and his becoming (*genomenos*) the cornerstone corresponds to his resurrection" (*The Hope of Israel*, 39).

And we are witnesses of all that he did both in the country of the Jews and in Jerusalem. They put him to death by hanging him on a tree, but God raised him on the third day and made him to appear, not to all the people but to us who had been chosen by God as witnesses, who ate and drank with him after he rose from the dead. (Acts 10:39–41).

Peter mentioned the third-day deliverance that Jesus experienced as well as the bodily appearances that followed it. Peter and the rest of the twelve had encountered the risen Christ. They ate with him as you would with an embodied person.

But Peter's proclamation about Jesus didn't end there. Peter told Cornelius that "he commanded us to preach to the people and to testify that he is the one appointed by God to be judge of the living and the dead" (10:42). While Jesus had been raised from the dead in the middle of history, a day would come when all the dead would rise to join the living. Peter's words are about the general resurrection that will impact all people, and he claimed Jesus is the appointed Judge. As Jesus taught in the Gospels, the future resurrection is associated with the final judgment.

Fulfilling Promises by Raising Jesus

Not only was God spreading the gospel of Christ through the ministry of Peter, he was also making Christ known through the apostle Paul. In a speech given to Jews in Pisidian Antioch, Paul said,

For those who live in Jerusalem and their rulers, because they did not recognize him nor understand the utterances of the prophets, which are read every Sabbath, fulfilled them by condemning him. . . . And when they had carried out all that was written of him, they took him down from the tree and laid him in a tomb. But God raised him from the dead, and for many days he appeared to those who had come up with him from Galilee to Jerusalem, who are now his witnesses to the people. (Acts 13:27, 29–31)

Paul framed the news of Jesus's resurrection the same way Peter did: Jesus had been rejected by Israel's leaders, God then vindicated him by resurrection, and this deliverance led to bodily encounters with his disciples. The act of raising Jesus was the fulfillment of divine promises. Paul said, "And we bring you the good news that what God promised to the fathers, this he has fulfilled to us their children by raising Jesus, as also it is written in the second Psalm, 'You are my Son / today I have begotten you'" (Acts 13:32–33). God had installed the Christ, the Son of David. Paul quoted from Isaiah 55:3 and Psalm 16:10 (see Acts 13:34–35) to demonstrate that the Davidic hopes had come to pass now in Jesus.[4] The body of Jesus did not see corruption (Acts 13:36–37). According to Crowe, "The lasting kingdom of David thus includes the benefit of eternal, resurrection life for those who are citizens of this kingdom. . . . The message of Pisidian Antioch is about the resurrection, both that of Christ and, by implication, the general resurrection."[5]

This message of forgiveness of sins through the risen Jesus is good news for everyone, because "everyone who believes is freed from everything from which you could not be freed by the law of Moses" (Acts 13:39). Paul then warned his hearers with the words of Habakkuk 1:5, saying,

> Look, you scoffers,
> be astounded and perish;

---

4. Crowe says, "Paul's speech is founded on the promise of the Davidic covenant (13:16–25), which is fulfilled by means of Jesus's resurrection (cf. 2 Sam. 7:12). God has delivered on his promise to David by raising Jesus from the dead" (*The Hope of Israel*, 54).

5. Crowe, *The Hope of Israel*, 56–57.

> for I am doing a work in your days,
>> a work that you will not believe, even if one tells it to
>>> you. (Acts 13:41)

Paul applied the words in Habakkuk 1:5 to the resurrection of Jesus. His hearers shouldn't scoff, lest they perish. They should trust the risen Jesus for the forgiveness of sins. Paul is the one who "tells it" to them.

If God has vindicated the Davidic King and installed him at his right hand, will these hearers now turn aside from this news?

The Necessity for the Christ to Rise

Paul's custom was to attend synagogue on the Sabbath day in order to demonstrate the truth of the Christian faith from the Old Testament. He kept to this custom when he entered Thessalonica. "And Paul went in, as was his custom, and on three Sabbath days he reasoned with them from the Scriptures, explaining and proving that it was necessary for the Christ to suffer and to rise from the dead, and saying, 'This Jesus, whom I proclaim to you, is the Christ'" (Acts 17:2–3).

When we read of Paul's evangelism in the synagogue, we are not told which Scriptures he used. Perhaps he drew from all of the Old Testament, showing from the Law and the Prophets and the Writings that the Messiah had to suffer and rise from the dead. Did he turn to Psalm 2 and herald Jesus as the anointed one who rules the nations? Did he open Psalm 16 and explain how David's words about a Holy One not seeing corruption were words about Jesus? Did he explain from Isaiah 53 how the suffering servant, though dying for our iniquities, would prolong his days and be vindicated? Did he quote from Genesis 22 where Isaac was delivered from death on the third day and then show the surpassing fulfillment of this type in the resurrection of Jesus?

We do not know which Old Testament passages Paul used in the synagogue, but over the course of three weeks he explained and demonstrated the necessity of Christ's suffering and resurrection.

Assurance of Jesus the Judge

In Athens, a city full of idols (Acts 17:16), Paul proclaimed the living God. He spoke of how God "made the world and everything in it," and that he "does not live in temples made by man" (17:24). The living God has no needs; in fact, he is the one who gives creatures breath and life and what they need (17:25). God's creation must know about an impending day of judgment.

Paul said, "The times of ignorance God overlooked, but now he commands all people everywhere to repent, because he has fixed a day on which he will judge the world in righteousness by a man whom he has appointed; and of this he has given assurance to all by raising him from the dead" (17:30–32). Like Peter had said to Cornelius (see 10:42), Jesus is the Judge of mankind. And according to Paul, God has made it clear that Jesus is the appointed Judge by the fact of his resurrection. God has "given assurance to all" that Jesus is the Judge of all the earth, "by raising him from the dead."

Sinners would be wise to ponder the implications if Jesus has indeed been raised from the dead.[6] Though the Greeks in Athens did not have hope for their own bodily resurrection, Paul was unashamedly proclaiming to them what the living God had done:

---

6. Crowe says, "The most important man for the Athenians to know about is neither Epicurus nor Zeno nor even Socrates—whose trial is recalled in Acts 17. Instead, the Athenians must regard the man who has been raised from the dead and will judge the entire world" (*The Hope of Israel*, 67).

a man died, was raised, and would judge the world in righteousness.[7] The resurrection of Jesus means all people should repent.

The Death and Resurrection of Eutychus

While Paul was ministering in Troas, he gave a long speech that lulled a young man to sleep. "Eutychus, sitting at the window, sank into a deep sleep as Paul talked still longer. And being overcome by sleep, he fell down from the third story and was taken up dead" (Acts 20:9). The death of Eutychus is the setup for a miraculous display of power through Christ's apostle.[8]

Paul went down and took Eutychus in his arms and said, "Do not be alarmed, for his life is in him" (20:10). This scene is a resurrection, where the deceased young man is revived in the arms of Paul. Like Peter in Acts 9 with Dorcas, and like Jesus raising people from the dead during his earthly ministry, Paul witnessed the return of life to a mortal body. Eutychus would one day die again. But a third-story fall during a lengthy Pauline speech would not be the last experience of Eutychus's earthly life.

The revival of Eutychus anticipates the final resurrection of the dead. This story in Acts 20, like the deliverances from death in the ministries of Elijah and Elisha, is a resurrection parable. While Eutychus slept and then died, we will all sleep the sleep of death. But in the arms of Christ, we will awake to new life.

---

7. According to N. T. Wright, "There is never any question what [Luke] believes about the final destiny of God's people: there will be a great day of judgment, at which Jesus, having himself been raised from the dead, will be the judge. At that time, all those who have believed in Jesus will be vindicated" (*The Resurrection of the Son of God*, Christian Origins and the Question of God, vol. 3 [Minneapolis: Fortress, 2003], 451).

8. Crowe suggests, "If Paul preached the resurrection and/or the ongoing reign of the risen Christ in his (lengthy) sermon in Troas (v. 7), then the raising of Eutychus may well have served as a sign of the spoken word" (*The Hope of Israel*, 73).

On Trial for the Resurrection of the Dead

After Paul had been arrested in Jerusalem, he stood before the council of Jewish leaders. He discerned that some members present were Pharisees and others Sadducees, so he said, "Brothers, I am a Pharisee, a son of Pharisees. It is with respect to the hope and the resurrection of the dead that I am on trial" (Acts 23:6).[9] The Pharisees affirmed a future resurrection while the Sadducees did not.

Paul's strategy was to poke at the theological tension between the Pharisees and Sadducees, yet his words were not false. He was indeed on trial with respect to "the hope and the resurrection of the dead." His message was that the resurrection of the dead had been inaugurated in Jesus of Nazareth, the one whom the Jewish leaders wanted crucified and the one whom God vindicated by raising him from the dead on the third day. Paul recognized the hope that had dawned with Jesus, and he both embraced it and heralded it.

A Resurrection of the Just and Unjust

At Caesarea the apostle Paul stands before Governor Felix and says,

> Knowing that for many years you have been a judge over this nation, I cheerfully make my defense. You can verify that it is not more than twelve days since I went up to worship in Jerusalem, and they did not find me disputing with anyone or stirring up a crowd, either in the temple or in the synagogues or in the city. Neither can they prove to you what they now bring up against me. (Acts 24:10–13)

---

9. According to C. Kavin Rowe, "From first to last, the Way is about the resurrection" (*World Upside Down: Reading Acts in the Graeco-Roman Age* [Oxford: Oxford University Press, 2009], 78).

After emphasizing his worshipful and peaceful presence in Jerusalem, Paul says,

> But this I confess to you, that according to the Way, which they call a sect, I worship the God of our fathers, believing everything laid down by the Law and written in the Prophets, having a hope in God, which these men themselves accept, that there will be a resurrection of both the just and the unjust. (24:14–15)

Moving backward through Paul's claim, he mentions a resurrection of "the just and the unjust." This alludes to Daniel 12:2, which promises that people will awake from the dust, some to everlasting life and others to everlasting shame and contempt. The religious leaders ("these men") believe this Scripture too and so have that same hope. Paul's hope is derived from the Scripture because he believes "everything laid down by the Law and written in the Prophets."

Paul's beliefs are what inform his hope. He hopes for a future resurrection because he believes what the Old Testament teaches. And as Scripture informs our hope through careful study of the Law, Prophets, and Writings, we see how reasonable and fitting it is that Paul looked for the day when the dead would rise.

The "just" referred to believers and the "unjust" to unbelievers. The "just" can only be considered such because of their trust in the Lord Jesus who becomes the righteousness that sinners need. But without faith in Jesus Christ, sinners have no righteousness to cover them on the last day. They are justly condemned as the "unjust."

The Incredible Thought of Resurrection

King Agrippa gave Paul permission to speak. Paul said, "My manner of life from my youth, spent from the beginning among my own nation and in Jerusalem, is known by all the Jews. They have known for a long time, if they are willing to testify, that according to the strictest party of our religion I have lived as a Pharisee" (Acts 26:4–5). Paul's life as a Pharisee means that he had held the beliefs of a Pharisee, and that included a hope in the resurrection of the dead. The irony, however, is that Paul's preaching about resurrection is what had led him to his trial before King Agrippa.

Paul said,

> And now I stand here on trial because of my hope in the promise made by God to our fathers, to which our twelve tribes hope to attain, as they earnestly worship night and day. And for this hope I am accused by Jews, O king! Why is it thought incredible by any of you that God raises the dead? (26:6–8)

Paul's question identifies the hope that has been inaugurated by Jesus Christ. The age of resurrection life has entered human history through the bodily vindication of Jesus from the dead.

Not only did Paul have a resurrection hope, but he says that the Jews' accusation against him pertains to this hope in Jesus that they reject. His accusers did not believe that Jesus is the resurrection and the life, nor did they affirm the bodily vindication of Jesus as the installment, or foreshadowing, of the resurrection for all God's people.[10] Paul did have this hope, and his hope for a future resurrection

---

10. David Peterson says, "The resurrection of the dead was no more believable in that context than it is for many in our so-called scientific age. . . . Yet, if the resurrection of Jesus took place, it challenges human skepticism about the possibility of encountering God and being judged by him. It is the best proof we have of a general resurrection and makes Jesus the key figure in God's plans for humanity" (*The Acts of the Apostles*, Pillar New Testament Commentary [Grand Rapids, MI: Eerdmans, 2009], 503).

was strengthened and made all the more sure by virtue of Christ's deliverance from death.

The accusers were misguided in their case against Paul because his hope is the same hope that the "twelve tribes" had and that the "fathers"—probably the patriarchs—before them had. The covenant-keeping God of life would fulfill his promises through the power of resurrection. Paul believed this hope was discernible in the Old Testament promises.[11]

Paul also affirmed that resurrection—even the resurrection of the one man Jesus—was not incredible when it comes to what God is able to do. His question is to the point: "Why is it thought incredible by any of you that God raises the dead?" (26:8). If people dismissed the idea of resurrection, they had not considered the scope of God's power or God's commitment to his promises. The empty tomb was a demonstration of God's power, and it was a further guarantee of the general hope of resurrection that the Old Testament promised.

The First to Rise from the Dead

Still before King Agrippa, the apostle Paul recounted his experience on the Damascus Road (Acts 26:12–18). Paul learned he had been persecuting Jesus by persecuting the followers of Jesus. His heaven-given mission was now to open the eyes of the spiritually blind, "so that they may turn from darkness to light and from the power of Satan to God, that they may receive forgiveness of sins" (26:18). It was for this mission that Paul had been seized by the Jews at the Jerusalem temple (26:21).

The mission and testimony of Paul had been undergirded by God's own power and preservation:

---

11. According to Crowe, "The hope that the fathers sought to attain (*katantesai*) has been confirmed, and indeed granted through the resurrection of Jesus. Jesus's resurrection does not contradict God's covenant promises, but fulfills what is anticipated night and day (26:7)" (*The Hope of Israel*, 80).

To this day I have had the help that comes from God, and so I stand here testifying both to small and great, saying nothing but what the prophets and Moses said would come to pass: that the Christ must suffer and that, by being the first to rise from the dead, he would proclaim light both to our people and to the Gentiles. (26:22–23)

Paul's message about the risen Jesus was in continuity with "what the prophets and Moses said would come to pass" (26:22). He asserted that the Old Testament, including the writings of Moses in the Law, foretold the suffering and vindication of God's promised Son (26:23). The light of Christ was for Jews and Gentiles—one Savior for all people. This fulfills the promise in Genesis 12:3, that through the family of Abraham "all the families of the earth shall be blessed."

The apostle specified that Jesus is "the first to rise from the dead" (Acts 26:23). This fact matters because the resurrection of Jesus did not mean a general resurrection was a misguided hope. Nor did Jesus's resurrection mean that others who died would follow suit in history and rise with glorified bodies a few days later. The future resurrection of the dead was a sure hope and now also an inaugurated one.

If someone read that Jesus was "the first to rise from the dead," he might wonder about Lazarus or the widow's son or Jairus's daughter. How was Jesus "the first" when these others preceded him? Or what about the people raised during the ministries of Elijah and Elisha? Didn't their deliverances precede Jesus's? Paul was aware of the Old Testament stories, and through his relationship with Luke he probably knew stories of how the lifegiving power of Jesus worked during Jesus's earthly ministry. Calling Jesus "the first to rise from the dead," then, was a deliberate emphasis on the kind of life that Jesus has, a life different from any deliverances that preceded.

Jesus was "the first to rise from the dead" because no previous deliverance led to embodied glory. Jesus was the first human being to put on the imperishable, to don immortality. Everyone else who came to life died again. The risen Jesus established the pattern of a new kind of existence. His resurrection carved the path that the dead would follow. He was "the first" of those whose new life would mean the death of death.

Conclusion

Jesus of Nazareth rose from the dead and brought into the present age the hope of resurrection life. According to the apostles in the book of Acts, this news about Jesus should be preached so that people may believe it. The message of the risen Christ provoked authorities and councils, yet the apostles knew that the righteous Judge of the earth superseded any political ranks and social influence around them. The resurrection of Jesus confirmed that he will be the Judge of the living and the dead. God raised his Son from death because he was keeping covenant promises. For these promises to be kept, death must be broken.

6

Resurrection Hope in the Letters

In the twenty-one New Testament Letters, resurrection hope is an important theme relevant to the gospel (for Christ has been raised from death) and to Christian living (for we look forward to our own bodies being raised). These letters exist because the tomb of Jesus is empty. The letter writers have different purposes in their documents and different emphases to their respective recipients, but the pervasive theme of resurrection hope cannot be missed.

Commissioned by the Risen Jesus

The apostle Paul writes as one who has encountered the Lord he once persecuted. On the road to Damascus, the risen and exalted Christ spoke to him and commissioned him for the mission of the gospel (Acts 9:1–19). Paul is unashamed to call himself a "servant of Christ Jesus" who "was declared to be the Son of God in power according to the Spirit of holiness by his resurrection from the dead" (Rom. 1:1, 4). The heavenly sonship of Jesus is announced and confirmed by the fact that the Father raised his Son.

Paul calls himself an apostle "not from men nor through man, but through Jesus Christ and God the Father, who raised him from the dead" (Gal. 1:1). Paul operated with the conviction that the authority of the risen Christ was decisive over his own life and ministry. If Jesus has been raised from the dead, then the proper role for Paul is being the servant and vessel of Christ to the nations.

Things of First Importance

Paul wrote to the Corinthians about teachings that ranked of "first importance" (1 Cor. 15:3). His letters contained many teachings and exhortations, but not everything was ranked with such primacy. He explained, "For I delivered to you as of first importance what I also received: that Christ died for our sins in accordance with the Scriptures, that he was buried, that he was raised on the third day in accordance with the Scriptures" (15:3–4).

The third-day resurrection of Jesus is integral to the traditions of "first importance" which Paul had received and was passing on to others. When Paul says that Jesus's resurrection was "in accordance with the Scriptures," he has in view not one particular text but a matrix of texts that prophesy or pattern the vindication and installment of God's Son. There are third-day deliverances, for example, in stories about Isaac, Hezekiah, Jonah, and Esther. And when you read of God promising to raise up a prophet like Moses (Deut. 18:18) and to raise up a son from David (2 Sam. 7:12–13), when you discern that the suffering servant will be vindicated (Isa. 53:10–12) and that the Davidic king will not experience bodily corruption (Ps. 16:10), the cumulative impression is that the biblical authors are laying the groundwork, the expectation, for the resurrection of Jesus on the third day.

No Gospel without Resurrection

The resurrection is so integral to the gospel that the good news is emptied of its power without it. There is no gospel worth believing or preserving if Jesus did not rise from the dead. Paul guides the Corinthians through a series of logical "if" statements:

> And if Christ has not been raised, then our preaching is in vain and your faith is in vain. We are even found to be misrepresenting God, because we testified about God that he raised Christ, whom he did not raise if it is true that the dead are not raised. For if the dead are not raised, not even Christ has been raised. And if Christ has not been raised, your faith is futile and you are still in your sins. Then those also who have fallen asleep in Christ have perished. If in Christ we have hope in this life only, we are of all people most to be pitied. (1 Cor. 15:14–19)

If Jesus were not raised, then death has defeated him, and he is not a victorious Savior. If the cords of death could not be loosed from his body, then we have no hope in him for our own resurrection.[1] If the tomb isn't empty, then the gospel is. But if Christ has been raised from the dead, then he charts a path of hope and glory that we will follow. If Christ has been raised from the dead, then our faith and labors are not in vain, and everyone who has died in Christ is secure (Rom. 8:31–39).

A Perpetual Priesthood

If Jesus did not rise from the dead, he cannot be the priest we need. Sinners need a Savior who can offer perpetual intercession, someone whose impeccable life and effective mediation will ensure that

---

1. According to L. Michael Morales, "He understood Jesus' resurrection from the dead, Jesus Christ himself, as God's utmost gift to humanity, the ultimate hope to which the hearts of God's people have always bent and the only possible—and profoundly logical—remedy for the great problem. Once the significance of Jesus' resurrection, and thus also of his sin-bearing crucifixion, had reached the full depths of his understanding, Paul realized that Jesus' resurrection was not only the redemption foretold in Scripture but the only real hope possible for the world" (*Exodus Old and New: A Biblical Theology of Redemption* [Downers Grove, IL: IVP Academic, 2020], 190).

sinners can approach the throne of grace with confidence. The resurrection of Jesus establishes his perpetual priesthood, thereby fulfilling the role occupied by the priestly mediators of Levi's tribe.

The writer of Hebrews notes that our great priest, the Lord Jesus, arises not from Levi's tribe but in the likeness of Melchizedek, and Jesus "has become a priest, not on the basis of a legal requirement concerning bodily descent, but by the power of an indestructible life. For it is witnessed of him,

> 'You are a priest forever,
>   after the order of Melchizedek.'" (Heb. 7:16–17)

Jesus is the priest we need because his resurrection life means that his priesthood will not cease. "The former priests were many in number, because they were prevented by death from continuing in office, but he holds his priesthood permanently, because he continues forever" (7:23–24).

The Firstfruits of the Resurrection

The teaching of Paul, consistent with the words of Jesus and the writings of the disciples, is that the future resurrection is a hope made more sure by the inauguration of resurrection life in Jesus. As the first to be raised in a glorified body, Jesus is "the firstfruits of those who have fallen asleep" (1 Cor. 15:20).

The word *firstfruits* is a harvest term. The arrival of a crop's firstfruits signals more to come. The resurrection of Jesus is the firstfruits of the general resurrection that is still to come. Jesus's defeat of death also confirms his supremacy. He is "the firstborn from the dead, that in everything he might be preeminent" (Col. 1:18). The order of embodied immortality is this: "Christ the firstfruits, then at his coming those who belong to Christ" (1 Cor. 15:23).

Defeat of the Last Enemy

Death is not something good in itself. While Paul says, "To live is Christ, and to die is gain" (Phil. 1:21), it is the greater communion with Christ that is gain. Death for the believer means to be absent from the body yet present with the Lord (2 Cor. 5:6–8). But the presence of death is a sign of sin's effects and abiding curse in the world (Rom. 5:12–13).

The death of God's image-bearers is a reminder that all is not right with the world. The resurrection of the dead would mean the defeat of death—the death of death. Christ reigns with glorified immortality at the right hand of the Father, and "he must reign until he has put all his enemies under his feet. The last enemy to be destroyed is death" (1 Cor. 15:25–26). The promise of resurrection is the promise to conquer death, the last enemy of God's people.

United with Him for Resurrection

Resurrection hope will be fulfilled for us because of our union with the already-risen Christ. Paul explains, "For if we have been united with him in a death like his, we shall certainly be united with him in a resurrection like his" (Rom. 6:5). And since we are united to Christ through faith, his victory over death will be ours at his return.[2]

Paul depicts our resurrection hope in a Christological way. Our resurrection will be "in a resurrection like his." Jesus is our example, our model, for the glorified life that bodily resurrection will bring. Paul says that Christ "will transform our lowly body to be like his glorious body, by the power that enables him even to subject all things to himself" (Phil. 3:21).

---

2. Constantine Campbell writes, "The point is clear: participation in death guarantees participation in resurrection" (*Paul and the Hope of Glory: An Exegetical and Theological Study* [Grand Rapids, MI: Zondervan, 2020], 168).

Raised with Christ Even Now

Our resurrection hope is not entirely future; our spiritual life in Christ has inaugurated it. The believer, in union with Christ, is alive to God in Christ. There is a spiritual transition from darkness to light, from death to life. We have been "raised with Christ" now (Col. 3:1). God has "raised us up" with Christ and "seated us with him in the heavenly places in Christ Jesus" (Eph. 2:6).

When we were dead in our trespasses and deserving of judgment, God showed mercy. "God made alive" the spiritually dead (Col. 2:13). This spiritual life is sourced in the lifegiving work of Christ's death, where he canceled the "record of debt that stood against us" and "disarmed the rulers and authorities" who opposed and accused us (2:14–15). Believers in Jesus have come to life. God has called to us through the powerful gospel and by his Spirit,

> Awake, O sleeper,
> > and arise from the dead,
> and Christ will shine on you. (Eph. 5:14)

Because we have been raised spiritually in Christ, we have already begun to "shine as lights in the world" (Phil. 2:15).[3] And, furthermore, "The resurrection of the body will be the fulfillment and completion of what has begun with spiritual resurrection."[4]

Future Resurrection and the Trinity

The believer will be raised from the dead, and this truth can be expressed in Trinitarian terms. Paul writes, "If the Spirit of him who

---

3. The language about shining "as lights in the world," paired with "holding fast to the word of life" (Phil. 2:15–16), alludes to Dan. 12:2–3, where we read that the dead will be raised and that the righteous/wise will shine. According to Phil. 2:15–16, this shining has been inaugurated by the spiritual life that we have in union with Christ. See Gordon D. Fee, *Paul's Letter to the Philippians*, New International Commentary on the New Testament (Grand Rapids, MI: Eerdmans, 1995), 246–47.

4. Campbell, *Paul and the Hope of Glory*, 197.

raised Jesus from the dead dwells in you, he who raised Christ Jesus from the dead will also give life to your mortal bodies through his Spirit who dwells in you" (Rom. 8:11). The believer has a mortal body until the resurrection. At that time, God will "give life" to the body and raise it.

In Paul's wording, the Father is "him who raised Jesus from the dead," and Paul says that if the Spirit of the Father dwells in you, then the Father who raised the Son will raise you as well. The writer of Hebrews implies the Father's raising of the Son near the end of the letter: "Now may the God of peace who brought again from the dead our Lord Jesus, the great shepherd of the sheep . . ." (Heb. 13:20). And as the great shepherd was raised, so shall his sheep be raised as well.

Glorified with Christ

The resurrection of the saints is their glorification. Paul says, "The Spirit himself bears witness with our spirit that we are children of God, and if children, then heirs—heirs of God and fellow heirs with Christ, provided we suffer with him in order that we may also be glorified with him" (Rom. 8:16–17).

Because we are heirs with Christ, we are heirs of glory, and our inheritance involves resurrection from the dead. This is ultimately how God conforms us to the image of his Son (Rom. 8:29).[5] Paul explains that those whom God predestined "he also called, and those whom he called he also justified, and those whom he justified he also glorified" (Rom. 8:30). The predestination of the saints ensures the glorification of the saints, and the pattern of their glorification is the risen Son. Through resurrection life and glory, we will "bear the image of the man of heaven" (1 Cor. 15:49).

---

5. Campbell says, "Putting these things together, Romans 8:29 indicates that conformity to the image of Christ is connected to resurrection, and it means that believers may be regarded as his siblings. . . . Sharing the image of Christ is bound up with resurrection from the dead and enables membership in the divine family" (*Paul and the Hope of Glory*, 180–81).

The Redemption of Our Bodies

We might rightly think of redemption as Christ's purchase of the saints for himself through his atoning work on the cross, but there is more to the language of redemption. Paul says, "For we know that the whole creation has been groaning together in the pains of childbirth until now. And not only the creation, but we ourselves, who have the firstfruits of the Spirit, groan inwardly as we wait eagerly for our adoption as sons, the redemption of our bodies" (Rom. 8:22–23).[6]

Our bodies will be redeemed through resurrection, and this too has been purchased and secured by Christ's work on the cross. The work of redemption will be thoroughly applied to us—not just to souls but to bodies. We have been wholly purchased and shall be wholly delivered. The redeeming work of Christ will not stop short of dealing with bodily death. Our future resurrection will be the culmination of our redemption.

Lord of the Dead and the Living

When Paul is explaining to the Roman Christians about conscience and not passing judgment on one another, he says,

> For none of us lives to himself, and none of us dies to himself. For if we live, we live to the Lord, and if we die, we die to the Lord. So then, whether we live or whether we die, we are the Lord's. For to this end Christ died and lived again, that he might be Lord both of the dead and of the living. (Rom. 14:7–9)

The resurrection of Christ is the cosmic assurance that he is Lord of all. Disciples belong to their risen Lord, and this doesn't change

---

6. According to Campbell, "*The redemption of our bodies* is naturally to be understood as bodily resurrection. Just as childbirth produces a living, breathing human being with an independent body, so creation will give birth to living, breathing human beings with independent, resurrected bodies. It is this prospect of future, bodily resurrection in which believers hope and for which they patiently wait" (*Paul and the Hope of Glory*, 171).

when they die. As the one who died and lives again, Jesus maintains unceasing lordship over his people. Our living and our dying, and eventually our living again, is all unto the Lord.

Our Behavior in the Body

The Christian life must be considered in light of our future resurrection. Because the body will be raised, the body matters. God's plan to raise the body confirms that he is committed to delivering it from the effects of sin and death. This resurrection hope should lead us to turn from sinful behaviors in this present age. Paul says, "The body is not meant for sexual immorality, but for the Lord, and the Lord for the body. And God raised the Lord and will also raise us up by his power. Do you not know that your bodies are members of Christ?" (1 Cor. 6:13–15).

As people joined to Christ by the Spirit, we cannot be indifferent about our bodily behavior.

> Let not sin therefore reign in your mortal body, to make you obey its passions. Do not present your members to sin as instruments for unrighteousness, but present yourselves to God as those who have been brought from death to life, and your members to God as instruments for righteousness. (Rom. 6:12–13)

If we have been raised in Christ spiritually, then we must live in a way that brings honor to God in our bodies which will be raised physically.

Present Sufferings and Coming Glory

All believers face suffering of various kinds. Paul made an astounding claim: "For I consider that the sufferings of this present time are not worth comparing with the glory that is to be revealed to us"

(Rom. 8:18). This greater glory is what God accomplishes through our resurrection from the dead, "the redemption of our bodies" (8:23). Resurrection power and glory is God's answer to the groaning of creation (8:19–22).

A resurrection hope helps us endure. Life is hard and trials are many, but glory is coming.

> So we do not lose heart. Though our outer self is wasting away, our inner self is being renewed day by day. For this light momentary affliction is preparing for us an eternal weight of glory beyond all comparison, as we look not to the things that are seen but to the things that are unseen. For the things that are seen are transient, but the things that are unseen are eternal. (2 Cor. 4:16–18)

Paul explains the unseen and eternal reality he has in mind in the next verse: "For we know that if the tent that is our earthly home is destroyed, we have a building from God, a house not made with hands, eternal in the heavens. For in this tent we groan, longing to put on our heavenly dwelling" (2 Cor. 5:1–2). The earthly tent is the mortal body, and resurrection from the dead will mean putting on the imperishable—the "building from God" that is "eternal."

All believers need encouragement to persevere through trials and sufferings, and Paul helps our perspective by highlighting the coming glory of resurrection life. We can have stronger resolve to endure bodily sufferings when we remember the hope we have of bodily redemption. Paul presses on with this perspective shaped by Christ's victory—"that I may know him and the power of his resurrection, and may share his sufferings, becoming like him in his death, that by any means possible I may attain the resurrection from the dead" (Phil. 3:10–11).[7]

---

7. According to Morales, "Surely this attaining of the resurrection of the dead is the greatest of all human quests, one for which any person would willingly sacrifice all else—for what does

Enduring with resurrection hope is also seen in Hebrews. The writer notes that followers of God faced suffering and hostility for their faith: "Some were tortured, refusing to accept release, so that they might rise again to a better life" (Heb. 11:35). This "better life" is resurrection life. Because the suffering saints had a resurrection hope, they endured their persecutors. Though their endurance may have meant earthly death, their future was glory—the "better life" of resurrection.

All Appearing at the Judgment Seat

The Son of God is the appointed Judge of the nations. And at his return the nations will be gathered for judgment through resurrection. Paul has this picture in view when he writes, "For we must all appear before the judgment seat of Christ, so that each one may receive what is due for what he has done in the body, whether good or evil" (2 Cor. 5:10).

Daniel 12:2 may have influenced Paul's language in 2 Corinthians 5:10 because there are two results at the judgment: some will receive their due for the good done in the body, while others will receive their due for the evil done in the body. The appearance of "all" is consistent with the expectation that the righteous and the unrighteous will be gathered for judgment.[8]

The words of Jesus in John 5 confirm that Paul is speaking about the future resurrection in 2 Corinthians 5:10. Jesus said that all those in the tombs will come out, "those who have done good to the resurrection of life, and those who have done evil to the resurrection of judgment" (John 5:29). The same notion may be meant in Romans 14:10, when

---

all else amount to when one's carcass is lowered into the earth? Cures for our sickness, precious though they are, are again but temporary remedies, for the body ages, it breaks down, and we must die and then face our Maker. But give us the guarantee of resurrection from the grave and the assurance that we are reconciled with God and suddenly all despair is pulled up by its roots. The resurrection from the dead: this is what is worth striving to attain if by any means" (*Exodus Old and New*, 193).

8. G. K. Beale says, "Both must be resurrected to receive their due in bodily form for what they had committed in their physical bodies" (*A New Testament Biblical Theology: The Unfolding of the Old Testament in the New* [Grand Rapids, MI: Baker Academic, 2011], 273).

Paul writes, "Why do you pass judgment on your brother? Or you, why do you despise your brother? For we will all stand before the judgment seat of God."[9] We rise to stand before God at the judgment seat.

The all-encompassing resurrection is also implied by the promise that the Lord will judge "the living and the dead." Paul writes, "I charge you in the presence of God and of Christ Jesus, who is to judge the living and the dead, and by his appearing and his kingdom: preach the word" (2 Tim. 4:1–2). If Christ will judge the dead, they will no longer be dead at the time of judgment. His judgment of the dead implies that he will give them bodily life. Peter warns that the wicked "will give account to him who is ready to judge the living and the dead" (1 Pet. 4:5). This, too, is a statement implying a general resurrection, when all will rise for judgment.

The Nature of the Resurrected Body

Taking the resurrection of Jesus as a pattern to inform our understanding of our own future resurrection, we can affirm that there is continuity: the body that dies is the body that rises. The gender of the dead person is preserved in resurrection life. There are fascinating questions about what a glorified body will be like, given that Jesus's resurrected body was capable of unusual acts (see Luke 24:31; John 20:19). But we must be content with some mystery for now.

As to insight about the nature of our resurrected bodies, Paul's words are a guide: "And what you sow is not the body that is to be, but a bare kernel, perhaps of wheat or of some other grain. But God gives it a body as he has chosen, and to each kind of seed its own

---

9. According to N. T. Wright, "The language of 'standing,' cognate with 'standing up', *anastasis*, and the emphasis that the master/lord has the power to 'make him stand', should almost certainly be taken as at least a sidelong reference to resurrection. At the last judgment, all must give an account of themselves, and the lord will 'make to stand', in other words, raise from the dead" (*The Resurrection of the Son of God*, Christian Origins and the Question of God, vol. 3 [Minneapolis: Fortress, 2003], 265).

body" (1 Cor. 15:37–38). The death of the body is a sowing, and the resurrection of the body is a reaping or harvesting of what was sown. Just as the final product of the seed is fitting with the kind of seed it is, the result of resurrection will be fitting for our existence as human image-bearers who are male and female.

Our future bodies will be immortal, incapable of dying again. Paul says, "What is sown is perishable; what is raised is imperishable. It is sown in dishonor; it is raised in glory. It is sown in weakness; it is raised in power. It is sown a natural body; it is raised a spiritual body" (1 Cor. 15:42–44). These verses describe our mortal existence under the sun. Our bodies are perishable. They are sown—or die— in dishonor because death is the defeat and humiliation of the body (see Eccles. 11:8; 12:1–8). The weakness of our bodies is evident in that we succumb to sickness, suffering, and death.

Since the body of Christ was raised imperishable, in glory, and in power, so will be our bodies at the coming resurrection.[10] "Just as we have borne the image of the man of dust, we shall also bear the image of the man of heaven" (1 Cor. 15:49). For now the in- carnate Son "alone has immortality" (1 Tim. 6:16), but because he "abolished death and brought life and immortality to light through the gospel" (2 Tim. 1:10), we will be raised with embodied im- mortality in him.

The Suddenness and Power of Resurrection

The impression from Paul's words is that the event of resurrection is sudden and powerful, not a drawn-out process of increasing con- formity. Paul says,

---

10. The language about the glory of this resurrected body may reflect Dan. 12:2–3, where the righteous would rise to everlasting life and shine like the stars. Richard Hays clarifies, "In Daniel, as in Paul's teaching, there is no thought that the risen righteous ones actually *become* stars; rather, the metaphor is used to suggest something about the glorious state they will enjoy when they rise from the dead" (*First Corinthians*, Interpretation [Louisville: John Knox, 1997], 271).

Behold! I tell you a mystery. We shall not all sleep, but we shall all be changed, in a moment, in the twinkling of an eye, at the last trumpet. For the trumpet will sound, and the dead will be raised imperishable, and we shall be changed. For this perishable body must put on the imperishable, and this mortal body must put on immortality. (1 Cor. 15:51–53)

The phrases "in a moment" and "in the twinkling of an eye" convey immediacy. Campbell says, "There will be no cocoon, hibernation, or somnolency. The event will therefore be one of transcendent power rather than naturally occurring processes."[11] Being "raised" and "changed" is the result of God's power bringing life to the dead. His divine power is so great that the perishable body is raised imperishable. God grants a kind of bodily life that will not end.

Resurrection at the Return of Christ

The apostle Paul explicitly connects the resurrection of the dead with Christ's return. "For the Lord himself will descend from heaven with a cry of command, with the voice of an archangel, and with the sound of the trumpet of God. And the dead in Christ will rise first" (1 Thess. 4:16). The language is reminiscent of 1 Corinthians 15:51–52.

The Lord's descent from heaven will fulfill the angelic promise in Acts 1:11: "Men of Galilee, why do you stand looking into heaven? This Jesus, who was taken up from you into heaven, will come in the same way as you saw him go into heaven." The ascension confirms the reign of the risen Christ, and his return will be to accomplish the resurrection and final judgment.

---

11. Campbell, *Paul and the Hope of Glory*, 183.

Punishment for the Wicked

Since Paul teaches that the return of Christ will involve the resurrection of the saints, what about the wicked? Their resurrection occurs at Christ's return, when all will gather at the judgment seat (2 Cor. 5:10). The Lord will be "revealed from heaven" (2 Thess. 1:7), Paul says,

> in flaming fire, inflicting vengeance on those who do not know God and on those who do not obey the gospel of our Lord Jesus. They will suffer the punishment of eternal destruction, away from the presence of the Lord and from the glory of his might, when he comes on that day to be glorified in his saints, and to be marveled at among all who have believed. (2 Thess. 1:8–10)

That Paul is talking about Christ's return is confirmed by language like "revealed from heaven" (1:7) and "when he comes on that day" (1:10). The judgment of the wicked is in view at Christ's return, for Paul says Christ will inflict vengeance (1:8), and the wicked will "suffer the punishment of eternal destruction" (1:9). This context is best situated in the general resurrection of the dead, as the righteous come to life for glory and the wicked rise for judgment. Paul's words announce the fulfillment of Daniel 12:2, that some people will awake to shame and everlasting contempt.[12]

The resurrection of the wicked will fulfill Paul's warning to the Galatians: "Do not be deceived: God is not mocked, for whatever one sows, that will he also reap. For the one who sows to his own flesh will from the flesh reap corruption, but the one who sows to the

---

12. Murray Harris says 2 Thess. 1:8–9 is a passage suggesting Paul's belief in a resurrection of the wicked unto condemnation ("Resurrection and Immortality in the Pauline Corpus," in *Life in the Face of Death: The Resurrection Message of the New Testament*, ed. Richard N. Longenecker [Grand Rapids, MI: Eerdmans, 1998], 151).

Spirit will from the Spirit reap eternal life" (Gal. 6:7–8). The wicked will reap bodily destruction.[13]

Salvation with Eternal Glory

As heirs of salvation, our inheritance includes glorification. Paul ministered with this hope: "Therefore I endure everything for the sake of the elect, that they also may obtain the salvation that is in Christ Jesus with eternal glory" (2 Tim. 2:10). Paul longed for all the saints to receive what God has prepared for them. This "salvation . . . with eternal glory" should be understood as resurrection life, reflecting the embodied glory that the risen Christ has now.

This understanding of 2 Timothy 2:10 is confirmed when Paul next writes a "trustworthy" saying: "If we have died with him, we will also live with him" (2 Tim. 2:11). This future life is unending, an experience of "eternal glory," which all the heirs of salvation will receive. This is our hope. For now we are to live "godly lives in the present age, waiting for our blessed hope, the appearing of the glory of our great God and Savior Jesus Christ" (Titus 2:12–13). The joy and glory of resurrection life is our blessed hope that our blessed Savior will bring us at his appearing.

Salvation Ready to Be Revealed

The believer can trust that the hardships of this world will not soil the glorious inheritance of the saints. We, the people of God, have been "born again to a living hope through the resurrection of Jesus Christ from the dead, to an inheritance that is imperishable, undefiled, and unfading, kept in heaven for you, who by God's power are being guarded through faith for a salvation ready to be revealed in the last time" (1 Pet. 1:3–5).

---

13. Thomas Schreiner says, "The contrast indicates that corruption refers to final destruction and final judgment" (*Galatians*, Zondervan Exegetical Commentary on the New Testament [Grand Rapids, MI: Zondervan, 2010], 369). See also Frank J. Matera, *Galatians*, Sacra Pagina (Collegeville, MN: Liturgical, 1992), 216.

The "salvation ready to be revealed" will be the culmination of God's work in us, the glorification of the saints. We have been born again for embodied immortality, and the trials of this life will not derail that destiny. Our inheritance is "imperishable, undefiled, and unfading," and those three descriptors will apply to us when Christ appears and raises the dead. As resurrected image-bearers, our bodies will be imperishable, our holiness undefiled, and our glory unfading.

In 1 John 3, the future hope we have is the result of God's love, making us his children. "Beloved, we are God's children now, and what we will be has not yet appeared; but we know that when he appears we shall be like him, because we shall see him as he is" (1 John 3:2). The appearing of Christ will mean the appearing of the glory we shall reflect in resurrected bodies. Beholding him, we shall be like him.

Conclusion

The New Testament letter writers proclaim the risen Christ and our hope to be raised with him. The suffering of the saints in this world will give way to greater glory, a life we were made for and will inherit. Christ has saved us from sin and will deliver us from all its effects, and that means the last enemy—death—will be defeated by our bodily resurrection. The empty tomb means that new creation has dawned. The firstfruits of resurrection life has been harvested, and this is the guarantee that God will bring all his children into embodied glory. For now we die, sowing our bodies in weakness and dishonor, down to the dust. But we sow in hope. What goes down must come up.

7

Resurrection Hope in Revelation

The reputation of Revelation precedes it. There is difficult imagery, the chapters are thick with Old Testament background, and scholars differ on how to understand even its most basic symbols. Despite the complexity of John's Apocalypse, we can join together in affirming two facts: Jesus is the glorified and risen one, and the future resurrection will accomplish both the bodily vindication of God's people and the bodily judgment of the wicked.

The Firstborn of the Dead

The apostle John writes the book of Revelation to seven churches in Asia Minor. In their letters, the apostles frequently pray for grace and peace from God to their recipients. John's unique wording goes like this: "Grace to you and peace from him who is and who was and who is to come, and from the seven spirits who are before his throne, and from Jesus Christ the faithful witness, the firstborn of the dead, and the ruler of kings on earth" (Rev. 1:4–5).

Among the phrases John ascribes to Jesus, he includes "the firstborn of the dead"—a resurrection claim. Other people in the Old and

New Testament stories came back to life, but they didn't rise to the glorified life that Jesus embodied. These other resurrections pointed to the hope of immortal physicality, the new kind of bodily life that Jesus inaugurated.

Jesus displays the new humanity, and as the head of new creation and the church, he is the representative and pioneer for everyone who now lives and dies in him. He is the firstborn not only "of the dead" but also of many brothers and sisters. Our risen elder brother, the firstborn, is the resurrection and the life.

The Keys of Death and Hades

The content of Revelation comes from John's visionary experience that begins with beholding the glorified Christ. The presence of Jesus is fearsome, awestriking, and overwhelming. He stood in John's vision like a priest with a long robe and sash around his waist (Rev. 1:13). He had white hair, eyes of fire, and feet like bronze (1:14–15). His voice was the thundering sound of many waters (1:15). He held seven stars in his right hand, and a sword protruded from his mouth (1:16). His face shone like the blazing sun (1:16).

Understandably, John was afraid and overcome by what he saw. But Jesus told him, "Fear not, I am the first and the last, and the living one. I died, and behold I am alive forevermore, and I have the keys of Death and Hades" (Rev. 1:17–18). Jesus is the "living one" because he was raised from the dead on the third day. He is the fountain of life and, as the living one, can grant life to others.

Jesus claimed to have "the keys of Death and Hades." First of all, this is a claim of authority. A key locks and unlocks, and the keyholder is someone with authority. Jesus is greater than death and hell. He has conquered them. By his death on the cross and his resurrection, he has broken the curse and neutralized the sting of death. Second, Jesus's words are a claim of access. He is the "living one";

death is no threat to him and could not hold him in the tomb. But he will also loose the pangs of death for his people. As the one with the keys, he will deliver the dead by resurrection.

Eating from the Tree of Life

In addressing the seven churches, John begins with the words of Jesus to Ephesus. The Ephesian saints have endured much, facing tests and evil, yet they have "abandoned the love [they] had at first" (Rev. 2:4). They must repent, lest Christ remove their lampstand (2:5). The Lord makes them a promise: "He who has an ear, let him hear what the Spirit says to the churches. To the one who conquers I will grant to eat of the tree of life, which is in the paradise of God" (2:7).

Conquering will come by repentance and faithfulness unto death. They must follow Christ even though it costs them. Their sacrifices, however, will not be in vain, because the saints of Christ will feast from the tree of life. They will experience the life that Adam and Eve were barred from (Gen. 3:22–24). The way to embodied immortality has been opened, and Jesus is the way and the life.

The tree of life is a symbol in Revelation 2:7 that should motivate the readers to endure. This tree is "in the paradise of God," which clearly evokes the garden of Eden (Gen. 2–3). When Jesus keeps his promise and the dead are raised to everlasting bodily life, it will not be merely a return to Eden but rather the culmination of everything the garden land anticipated. If the Ephesian saints remember the incomparable hope of the glory to come, they will conquer. And as conquerors, they will feast in the paradise of God.

The Crown of Life

The church in Smyrna had faced tribulation and poverty (Rev. 2:9). Persecutors caused suffering, and there was more to come. Jesus tells them, "Do not fear what you are about to suffer. Behold, the devil is about to throw some of you into prison, that you may be tested, and for ten days you will have tribulation. Be faithful unto death, and I will give you the crown of life" (Rev. 2:10).

The believers faced the possibility of physical suffering. Jesus tells them, in a way different from Paul yet still with the same message, that their present sufferings are not worth comparing to the glory that will be revealed (Rom. 8:18). Faithfulness to death will lead to life. The image of a "crown" in Revelation 2:10 denotes victory and royalty. During the race of their Christian lives, these believers in Smyrna would be tempted to defect from Christ, to compromise their faithfulness to him out of self-preservation. Jesus tells them, "Do not fear" (2:10). They need a hope that is greater than fear. They need to think about their sovereign Christ and the crown of life he bestows on his people.

The crown of life is the hope for the overcomer. Death may come, but greater life will follow. Believers will reign with Christ. Faithfulness on earth may result in prison, but the prisoners will reign. Faithfulness on earth may lead to suffering and death, but the dead will live. This hope is what Jesus meant in Mark 8:35: "For whoever would save his life will lose it, but whoever loses his life for my sake and the gospel's will save it."

The Second Death

Everyone will die once, but some will die twice. There is a second death in the book of Revelation, and it relates to the final judgment of the wicked. In Jesus's words to the believers in Smyrna, he says, "He who has an ear, let him hear what the Spirit says to the churches. The one who conquers will not be hurt by the second death" (Rev. 2:11).

The "second death" is the everlasting judgment of resurrected unbelievers. It is a death that never ends, parallel to the future unending life of the saints. This death is called "second" because the first death is the ending of earthly life. And it is called "death" because the future of the wicked is the opposite of hope, flourishing, and peace. At the return of Christ, the wicked will be raised for the second death.

The promise in 2:11 is that "the one who conquers will not be hurt by the second death." Believers can take comfort, then, that any sufferings in this life will not extend into the life to come. The saints will have but one death. Blessed are the saints who are faithful unto death, for theirs is the crown of life. But woe to those who refuse Christ and love this world, for theirs is the second death.

Authority and the Morning Star

Sometimes there are promises that can only come to fruition in a context of embodied life. Jesus's words to the believers in Thyatira are an example of such promises. We know that Jesus is the Son of David, the anointed one, who reigns over the nations and whose sovereign word will overcome his enemies. He is the King of Psalm 2. In a life of embodied glory, the risen Christ has a kingdom that will never end.

Knowing these things about Jesus, we can read with amazement what Jesus promises the saints in Thyatira:

> Only hold fast what you have until I come. The one who conquers and who keeps my works until the end, to him I will give authority over the nations, and he will rule them with a rod of iron, as when earthen pots are broken in pieces, even as I myself have received authority from my Father. And I will give him the morning star. (Rev. 2:25–28)

Jesus is saying that the conquerors will reign with him. He is extending the realities of Psalm 2:8–9 beyond himself and to his people who are heirs with him. In union with Christ, the people of

Christ will be given authority and rule. The "morning star" (Rev. 2:28) may refer to Christ himself (see Num. 24:17) or perhaps to the shining glory that corresponds to future resurrection life (see Dan. 12:3). Jesus's promises are at least indirectly about the resurrection, for the saints anticipate having the same kind of life as their Savior in the everlasting kingdom.[1] They cannot reign with Christ fully if they remain defeated by death.

The Reputation of Being Alive

To the church in Sardis, Jesus gives an exhortation to wake up. Their condition is not hidden from God, and they need to demonstrate the spiritual life they claim to have and that others say they have.

> I know your works. You have the reputation of being alive, but you are dead. Wake up, and strengthen what remains and is about to die, for I have not found your works complete in the sight of my God. Remember, then, what you received and heard. Keep it, and repent. If you will not wake up, I will come like a thief, and you will not know at what hour I will come against you. (Rev. 3:1–3)

Godly repentance is a sign of life. The church in Sardis needed spiritual awakening that is in sync with those who have been brought from death to life. Their spiritual resurrection in Christ should bear the fruit of repentance and obedience. If those who claim to be alive—and have the reputation of being alive—refuse to keep the words of Christ and manifest the fruit of the Spirit, then they will face Jesus Christ the righteous Judge. He will come against them (3:3).

---

1. As Brian Tabb explains, "These promises function as incentives and invitations for embattled believers to persevere in following Christ and share in the inheritance in the New Jerusalem" (*All Things New: Revelation as Canonical Capstone*, New Studies in Biblical Theology [Downers Grove, IL: IVP Academic, 2019], 110).

Spiritual resurrection, which is what happens when the believer is united to Christ by the Spirit through faith, is lifegiving and productive. How could a genuine union with the risen Christ be paired with an unrepentant life? How could the powerful Spirit of God indwell a believer and yet that person live as if spiritually dead?

The words of Jesus to the saints in Sardis are a wakeup call. The people of Jesus have been raised with him spiritually and will be raised with him physically. The infusion of life into our dead hearts means we are now alive to God in Christ, so we must live as those who are awake.[2]

The Slain Lamb Standing

John sees the enthroned one holding a scroll with seven seals that no one could open (Rev. 5:1–3). When John wept loudly, one of the elders told him, "Weep no more; behold, the Lion of the tribe of Judah, the Root of David, has conquered, so that he can open the scroll and its seven seals" (5:5). John looked and saw "a Lamb standing, as though it had been slain" (5:6).

The converging images make a powerful point. The elder spoke of the Lion from Judah's tribe, yet when John turned to see this mighty one, he saw a Lamb. This Lamb was standing, yet it had been slain. The standing position must mean the Lamb's vindication. The Lamb had been slain, but now it was slain no more. The Lamb is the Lion of Judah's tribe, and he "has conquered" (5:5).

Interpreters can connect these images to the Lord Jesus. He was the Lamb of God given for the sins of the world, slain on the cross. And as the promised King from Judah's tribe, he was vindicated through his resurrection so that he might ascend and reign with

---

2. Paul puts the truth this way in Romans: "So you also must consider yourselves dead to sin and alive to God in Christ Jesus. Let not sin therefore reign in your mortal body, to make you obey its passions" (Rom. 6:11–12).

immortal physicality. Sufferers can rejoice that their Savior has conquered sin and death, and his life and reign will be theirs. He has conquered, and they will conquer in him.

Two Witnesses and the Breath of God

John learns about two witnesses who receive authority and prophesy (Rev. 11:3–6). These figures will hold to their testimony unto death, killed by the beast (11:7).

> For three and a half days some from the peoples and tribes and languages and nations will gaze at their dead bodies and refuse to let them be placed in a tomb, and those who dwell on the earth will rejoice over them and make merry and exchange presents, because these two prophets had been a torment to those who dwell on the earth. (11:9–10)

John does not learn the identities of these two witnesses, but they may represent the confessing church of Christ which faces persecution for the gospel.[3] Regardless, the two witnesses are vindicated by resurrection:

> But after the three and a half days a breath of life from God entered them, and they stood up on their feet, and great fear fell on those who saw them. Then they heard a loud voice from heaven saying to them, "Come up here!" And they went up to heaven in a cloud, and their enemies watched them. (Rev. 11:11–12)

The vindication of these witnesses included both resurrection and ascension! The breath of life entered their bodies, which is reminis-

---

3. The reason these two witnesses may symbolize the church is that they are called "two lampstands" in Rev. 11:4, and lampstands are identified with churches in 1:20. See Tabb, *All Things New*, 97–101.

cent of Ezekiel 37:1–14, when God's breath enlivened the bodies in the prophet's vision.

God's deliverance of the two witnesses in Revelation 11 foreshadows the future life of the saints. Though Christians may face opposition and even death for their adherence to the gospel, they will rise from the dead and reign with the Savior.

> John's vision of the two witnesses stresses that life, not the suffering and death, is the final word for followers of the Lamb. After a period of difficulty and seeming defeat, the living God will decisively vindicate believers and raise them from the dead by his life-giving Spirit, following the pattern of their resurrected Lord who now holds the keys of Death and Hades (1:18).[4]

The breath of God will overrule their accusers.

The First Resurrection

Among the controversial chapters in Revelation, none is more so than Revelation 20.[5] In John's vision, the devil was bound and thrown into a pit so that he might not deceive the nations, until a thousand years ended (Rev. 20:3).

> Then I saw thrones, and seated on them were those to whom the authority to judge was committed. Also I saw the souls of those who had been beheaded for the testimony of Jesus and for the word of God, and those who had not worshiped the beast or its image and had not received its mark on their

---

4. Tabb, *All Things New*, 76.
5. The opening verses in Rev. 20 use the "thousand years" language (20:2, 3, 4, 5, 6, 7) that interpreters divide over. For an explanation of different millennial positions, see Thomas R. Schreiner, *The Joy of Hearing: A Theology of the Book of Revelation* (Wheaton, IL: Crossway, 2021), 161–78.

foreheads or their hands. They came to life and reigned with Christ for a thousand years. (20:4)

John saw people who had died because of their faithfulness to Christ. He saw their "souls," so they were disembodied. And they "came to life and reigned with Christ." The expression "came to life" is explained by "reigned with Christ." This reigning with Christ in heaven is what John means by the "first resurrection" (20:5). A first resurrection points to a second. Just as the "second death" denotes everlasting bodily judgment, a first resurrection looks toward a second resurrection that denotes everlasting bodily life. The saints will have an embodied reign in union with the risen and glorified Christ.

The Dead Standing before the Throne

The vision of John depicts the final judgment when the dead are raised and all are gathered before "a great white throne" (Rev. 20:11).

> And I saw the dead, great and small, standing before the throne, and books were opened. Then another book was opened, which is the book of life. And the dead were judged by what was written in the books, according to what they had done. And the sea gave up the dead who were in it, Death and Hades gave up the dead who were in them, and they were judged, each one of them, according to what they had done. (20:12–13)

John saw the dead "standing," and they stood because they had been raised. Just as Jesus and the apostles taught in the Gospels and in the Letters, the resurrection of the dead and the final judgment go together. The dead come to life in order for the Lord to establish their respective everlasting embodied states.[6] The wicked will experience the warning given by John: "And if anyone's name was not found written in the book of life, he was thrown into the lake of fire" (Rev. 20:15; see also 21:8). The book of life designates those whose future is life. A name not in the book of life will have a future of death—the second death.

Death and Other Former Things

The righteous will dwell with the Lord in a new heaven and new earth (Rev. 21:1). The former things of this fallen world will pass away. God "will wipe away every tear from their eyes, and death shall be no more, neither shall there be mourning, nor crying, nor pain anymore, for the former things have passed away. And he who was seated on the throne said, 'Behold, I am making all things new'" (21:4–5).

The plan to make "all things new" encompasses the reality of death. Ever since the events of Genesis 3, death has been part of the human story. According to Kelly Kapic,

> Christian affirmation of resurrection is not chiefly about escaping this world but righting it. Resurrection is not about denying this world but rather enabling believers to have an honest assessment of their experience and yet to have a real hope for restoration beyond it. Pain is real, but it is not the only reality.[7]

The conquest over sin and its effects will include the defeat of death and the things associated with the forces of death—mourning,

---

6. The prophecy in Dan. 12:2 is fulfilled in Rev. 20:12–13.
7. Kelly M. Kapic, *Embodied Hope: A Theological Meditation on Pain and Suffering* (Downers Grove, IL: IVP Academic, 2017), 115.

crying, and pain. This hope is based in Isaiah 25:8 where the prophet says,

> He will swallow up death forever;
> and the Lord GOD will wipe away tears from all faces,
> and the reproach of his people he will take away
> from all the earth,
> for the LORD has spoken."

In John's vision the victory of God is made complete. The wicked have been condemned, the righteous have been vindicated, and the covenant faithfulness of God will be the unending portion of his people.

The reason "death shall be no more" is because the tombs will be emptied and everlasting states established. With all bodies dwelling in either embodied glory or embodied shame, there will be no more physical death.

Leaves of the Tree of Life

In the last chapter of Scripture, we once again see the tree of life, first mentioned in Genesis 2–3. "References to the tree of life in the midst of paradise in Genesis 2–3 and Revelation 22 create an inclusio framing the entire biblical story."[8] Barred from access to that tree, Adam and Eve dwelled outside of Eden and died. This tree held forth the promise of embodied immortality, something that resurrection life would ensure. In Revelation 22 we read,

> Then the angel showed me the river of the water of life, bright
> as crystal, flowing from the throne of God and of the Lamb
> through the middle of the street of the city; also, on either

---

8. Tabb, *All Things New*, 189.

side of the river, the tree of life with its twelve kinds of fruit,
yielding its fruit each month. The leaves of the tree were for
the healing of the nations. (Rev. 22:1–2)

John's vision reveals an unending supply of life and healing for
the nations, represented by the tree of life bearing fruit each month.
Access to the tree is emphasized by its mysterious placement on each
side of the river. Whereas in Genesis 3:22–24 Adam and Eve were
barred from this tree, in Revelation 22 the nations will feast on its
fruit. These nations are believers from every tribe and tongue, who
trust in Christ and follow him as disciples. This Christian identity
is what Revelation 22:14 means: "Blessed are those who wash their
robes, so that they may have the right to the tree of life and that they
may enter the city by the gates."

The wicked will not feast from the tree of life. They will remain
alienated from the blessings and favor of God. Their only hope in
this life is to cast themselves on God's mercy in Christ Jesus, that they
might find pardon and life before the day of judgment. The words in
the book of Revelation are so important that "if anyone takes away
from the words of the book of this prophecy, God will take away his
share in the tree of life and in the holy city, which are described in
this book" (Rev. 22:19). Readers should believe and heed what John
has said and what Jesus has said through him.

Conclusion

The slain Lamb has conquered death, and we will conquer death in
him. Though Christians around the world will face hostility and even
death for their faith, theirs is the crown of life. Physical death will
give way to being with Christ, and the return of Christ will bring to
pass the resurrection of the dead. The embodied glory of the righteous will be manifested in a new creation where they will dwell

with God, and God with them. The unrighteous will face the second death, the unending punishment that includes the devil and his rebel angels. If we know and love the sovereign Christ, we need not fear, for he himself is the living one who holds the keys to death and Hades. Life and glory are his to give, and they will be ours to receive.[9]

9. According to Constantine Campbell, "The glory of Christ is also hidden in the present age, though it can be seen by those with eyes to see it. He is the Lord of glory, he has been raised in glory and in a glorious body, and he is the hope of glory. The glory of God is seen in Christ, and when he appears in glory those hidden with him will appear with him in glory. Though the glory of God is inherent in his own being and manifested in Christ, it is shared with believers, who have been called by God into his kingdom and glory. Though believers will ascribe glory to Christ when he comes, they will also partake in his glory" (*Paul and the Hope of Glory: An Exegetical and Theological Study* [Grand Rapids, MI: Zondervan Academic, 2020], 461).

Conclusion

According to the whole counsel of Scripture, believers can have hope that their covenant-making God will keep his promises and overcome the forces of death in this world. The Lord Jesus shows the way. His power subdued the effects of sin and death in the lives of others during his earthly ministry. And his own resurrection from the dead serves as the pattern for the future life and glory of God's people. Because of our union with Christ, we live and will live.

Tracking the development of resurrection hope in God's Word is not a simple task. The New Testament teachings about future embodied life are rooted in Old Testament stories and prophecies. The roots go deep, all the way back to Genesis. The importance of resurrection is tied to the kind of existence God gave to Adam and Eve. Since they were image-bearers with bodies, the redemption of sinners will include giving life to dead bodies as well.

The God of life is at work throughout the Old Testament, opening wombs, liberating captives, rescuing the helpless, and overcoming illness—pushing back the forces of death with irresistible power. These mighty acts of God are fuel for hope that the cords of death are weaker than they appear and will actually burst because of the expulsive strength of new creation. The Law, Prophets, and Writings join together to say, "Death shall surely die."

In the New Testament, Jesus of Nazareth, the long-awaited seed of the woman, bore sin's curse and conquered death. He arose the firstborn of new creation. And he ascended to reign, one day to return. The second coming of Christ will accomplish the consummation of the work he inaugurated. The dead will be raised, with the righteous vindicated and the wicked condemned.

Our hope of glory can help us endure this present age, where enemies of the cross rage like the dragon they follow. We cannot fully fathom the glory that is coming, but God will raise us up so that we can receive it. We walk through the valley of the shadow of death as heirs of an everlasting kingdom. Only embodied immortality will fit with such a place.

From the dust we will rise to reign. No more exile, no more corruption, no more loss—all things will be made new. For now, every graveyard is a garden, awaiting the reaping of what is sown. From the dust we will rise to shine, like stars in a new creation. We will display a glory and life flowing forever from our unbreakable union with Christ. All will be well.

For Further Reading

For further study on the topic of resurrection hope, I commend the following resources.

Crowe, Brandon. *The Hope of Israel: The Resurrection of Christ in the Acts of the Apostles*. Grand Rapids, MI: Baker Academic, 2020.

Dempster, Stephen G. "From Slight Peg to Cornerstone to Capstone: The Resurrection of Christ on 'The Third Day' According to the Scriptures." *Westminster Theological Journal* 76 (2014): 371–410.

Hays, Richard B. "Reading Scripture in Light of the Resurrection." Pages 216–239 in *The Art of Reading Scripture*. Edited by Ellen F. Davis and Richard B. Hays. Grand Rapids, MI: Eerdmans, 2003.

Kapic, Kelly. *Embodied Hope: A Theological Meditation on Pain and Suffering*. Downers Grove, IL: IVP Academic, 2017.

Levenson, Jon. *Resurrection and the Restoration of Israel: The Ultimate Victory of the God of Life*. New Haven, CT: Yale University Press, 2006.

Morales, L. Michael. *Exodus Old and New: A Biblical Theology of Redemption*. Downers Grove, IL: IVP Academic, 2020.

Vos, Geerhardus. *The Eschatology of the Old Testament*. Edited by James T. Dennison, Jr. Phillipsburg, NJ: P&R, 2001.

Wright, N. T. *The Resurrection of the Son of God*. Volume 3 of Christian Origins and the Question of God. Minneapolis: Fortress, 2003.

General Index

Aaron, 81
Abednego, 74
abhorrence, 53n13
Abraham, 18, 27, 28–29, 39, 90, 102
Absalom, 46
Adam, 22–23, 24, 25, 135, 144, 145, 147
Agrippa, 111, 112
Alexander, T. D., 21n1
alienation, 24, 82, 145
allusion, 29n12, 75, 84, 87, 110, 120
Anderson, Bernard W., 63n2
Asaph, 65–67
ascension, 97–98, 140
authority, 134, 137–38

Babylonian captivity, 24n7, 55, 76
baptism, 26
barrenness, 27, 39, 40, 43
Bauckham, Richard, 61n1
Beale, G. K., 53n12, 84n5, 125n8
beatific vision, 63
behavior, 123
blessing, 51, 58, 68
blindness, 52, 81
Boaz, 71
bodies
   behavior of, 123
   burial of, 30–31
   as perishable, 22

redemption of, 57, 122
   as resurrected, 126–27
bones
   burying in Canaan, 30–31
   coming alive, 54–55
   of Elisha, 48–49
bringing up, 65
Bronner, Leila, 37n18
burial, 30–31

Campbell, Constantine, 119n2, 121n5, 122n6, 128, 146n9
Canaan, 30–31
childlessness, 27. *See also* barrenness
Christian living, 115
Christology, 19, 119
conquest, 42
continuity, 95, 126
Cornelius, 103–4, 107
cornerstone, 102–3
corporate resurrection, 76
covenant, 41, 90, 112, 114, 147
covenant curses, 67
covenant faithfulness, 46
creation, 26–27, 52
critical scholarship, 21n1
Crowe, Brandon, 90n11, 102n2, 103n3, 105, 105n4, 107n6, 108n8, 112n11

Obed, 71
obedience, 138
Old Testament, 17–19, 110, 112, 147
Osborne, Grant, 88n9

parable of the weeds, 86
patriarchs, 27, 39, 42, 90, 112
Paul
    commissioning, of, 115–16
    on Old Testament resurrection,
        37–38
    on resurrection, 105
    at the synagogue, 106–7
Pentateuch, 38
Pentecost, 98
persecution, 125, 135, 140
Peter, 62, 98–104
Peterson, David, 111n10
Pharaoh, 29
Pharisees, 109, 111
physical death, 24
Plato, 22n2
predestination, 121
priesthood, as perpetual, 117–18
promises, 41
prophet, 35
Prophets, 17, 38, 41–60, 110
punishment, 129–30

Rachel, 27
Rebekah, 27
rebellion, 26
reconciliation, 103
redemption, 122
Rehoboam, 44
relationships, 19
repentance, 55, 56, 135, 138
rescue, 60
restoration, 56, 70–71, 80–81, 143
resurrection
    faith of, 28
    firstfruits of, 79, 118, 131
    as future, 120–21

to judgment, 75
of just and unjust, 109–10
as liberation, 32
marriage at, 89
necessity of, 106–7
in the Old Testament, 17–19
repayment at, 88–89
at return of Christ, 128
suddenness of, 127–28
as teaching of first importance, 116
reversal, 43, 51, 73
reviving, 65
righteous, 77, 86
righteousness, 70
ritual impurity, 91n12
Rowe, C. Kavin, 109n9
Ruth, 71

Sadducees, 38–39, 89, 90, 109
salvation, 130
Sarah, 27, 30
Sardis, 138
Saul, 46
Schreiner, Thomas, 83n4, 130n13
second death, 136–37, 143, 146
separation, 24, 25n8, 86
Sermon on the Mount, 87
sexual immorality, 123
Shadrach, 73–74
shame, 24, 75
Sheol, 44, 46, 56–57, 61–63, 64, 99
shining, 120n3
Shunammite's son, 47–48
sickness, 127
sin, 24, 26, 56, 60
skin disease, 34
slavery, 40
sleep, 51, 92
Smyrna, 135, 136
Solomon, 44, 70
soul sleep, 51n9
spiritual darkness, 41
spiritual resurrection, 120, 138–39

Scripture Index

Short Studies in Biblical Theology Series

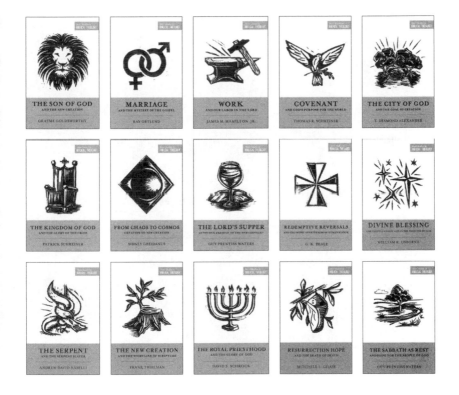

For more information, visit **crossway.org/ssbt**.